GENERATIVE COACHING
Volume 3
Multiple levels of creating success

International Association for Generative Change

114 Ponderosa Drive

Santa Cruz, CA 95060

USA

Email: info@generative-change.com

Homepage: https://generative-change.com/

Library of Congress Control Number: 2021907725

I.S.B.N. 979-8-218-15622-0

Generative Coaching

GENERATIVE COACHING
Volume 3
Multiple levels of creating success

Robert B. Dilts

Stephen Gilligan

Design and Illustrations by Antonio Meza

TABLE OF CONTENTS

TABLE OF CONTENTS

TABLE OF CONTENTS

Dedication

We dedicate this volume to Stephen's granddaughter River, Robert's grandnephew Cyrus, and Antonio's daughter Luz Carmen. May this new generation continue to guide us to creative and sustainable change.

Acknowledgments

We would like to acknowledge our sponsors over the years who have supported the development of our Generative Coaching work and provided a platform for us to share it with so many others. Special thanks go to Richard and Oksana Konner who sponsored the program from which many of the examples presented in this volume were taken.

We also want to acknowledge the many students who have participated in helping us evolve this work. Particular gratitude goes to those who participated in the demonstrations presented in this volume.

We additionally want to acknowledge all of the members of the International Association for Generative Change who have joined us in bringing this dream to a reality. These members include our fellow teachers, professional members, associate members and other participants in the IAGC community who are as passionate about the work as we are.

Acknowledgment also goes to Michele Roush, who did the important job of proofreading this volume

Last, and certainly not least. we are especially grateful to Antonio Meza who has done the spectacular illustrations for this series. We continue to be astonished and impressed with Antonio's versatility and his genius in visually capturing not only our message, but the spirit of Generative Change from which it comes. As with the previous volumes of *Generative Coaching*, Antonio's drawings bring the work alive in ways that the written word cannot possibly accomplish.

Preface

In the years since 2010, when we did our very first Generative Coaching program, the need for generative change has become increasingly clear and urgent. There are many, many reasons that humanity cannot keep doing things as we have done in the past. We all live in a global ecosystem that is rapidly changing and that poses both opportunities and dangers that cannot be effectively addressed with the actions and same ways of thinking that have been used before.

The processes and prototypes of Generative Coaching were developed to support people to explore how to achieve new things in new ways. This third volume of the **Generative Coaching** series encompasses the material that we generally cover in the third module of our Generative Coaching Certification program. This module is usually done by Robert, who will be the main voice in this book, as Steve's was for **Volume 2**.

Creating and managing ecological and sustainable change is a multilevel process. Changing our actions involves changing our mind and mindset. This includes increasing our knowledge and know-how, but it also frequently requires a shift in our priorities and motivations as well. Sometimes it means updating even deeper processes, such as our perceptions of our identity and our sense of purpose.

A major theme in this volume is the role that beliefs play in either supporting or inhibiting creativity. Deeply held beliefs weave together all three of the areas that make up our consciousness—cognitive, somatic and field. These three domains of experience have a powerful influence on the way we build our realities. In the coming pages, we will be showing how we can strengthen empowering beliefs as well as identify and transform belief barriers that can disempower us or hold us back.

Another important theme in **Volume 3** is how to adapt Generative Coaching principles and procedures to a virtual environment. New developments in technology have made online coaching a common and, at times, necessary option. It has been a pleasant surprise to both of us to discover that Generative Coaching can be so readily and effectively adapted to the context of a virtual environment.

If you have read the first two volumes of *Generative Coaching*, our hope is that this book will help you to take your coaching practice to another level. If this is your first exploration of Generative Coaching, may it be an exciting and valuable experience for you and may it open the door to a new approach to create a better and more fulfilling future for yourself and others.

Robert Dilts and Stephen Gilligan

May my mind come alive today
To the invisible geography
That invites me to new frontiers,
To break the dead shell of yesterdays,
To risk being disturbed and changed.

May I have the courage today
To live the life that I would love,
To postpone my dream no longer
But do at last what I came here for
And waste my heart on fear no more.

—from *A Morning Offering*
by John O'Donohue

Chapter 1

Introduction and Overview

In Volume 3 of *Generative Coaching*, we will continue to deepen and enrich the foundations of generative change and each of the six steps of the generative coaching process. We will be adding more nuances and possibilities to our basic prototypes. While it would be, of course, helpful to have read the first two volumes, it is not necessary in order to learn and benefit from this third volume. In fact, in this opening chapter we are going to begin with a review of the basic principles of generative change and the six-step model of Generative Coaching. Then, in the coming chapters, we will present some other ways of doing those steps. For instance, we will be introducing the role that beliefs play in the generative coaching process. We will also be examining how to do generative coaching virtually.

The Increasing Need for Generative Change

As we have pointed out in our previous volumes, generative change means to create something new or to do something in a completely new way. Generative change is necessary when you can no longer keep doing what has been done before; either because it is not possible or because it doesn't work anymore. As we look around at the challenges we face in our world today, it seems obvious that generative change is needed as much or more now than any other time in human history. In both big and small ways, we need to do things differently.

Generativity is also necessary to effectively deal with the new obstacles that continue to emerge in our changing world. We are constantly facing unprecedented challenges that affect our health, our livelihoods, our careers, our relationships with others, and our relationship with our planet.

A coach was originally a vehicle that transported people from some present state to a desired state

A "coach" is literally a vehicle that takes you from some present state to some desired state. Generative Coaching is about helping ourselves and others move from our present states to desired states that have not previously existed. Generative Coaching is also needed when we have to create a whole new path to get to a desired state that we've gotten to before but can no longer do in the same way. In today's world, we need both of those—to achieve new things, and also to achieve things in new ways. Not only are we needing and wanting to go somewhere new, but we also have to get there using novel approaches. This is why, in Generative Coaching, we express our desired state in the form of an intention to create something rather than as a determination to achieve a specific objective in a particular way. When we begin a journey of generative change, we cannot know all of the details of either the path or the destination.

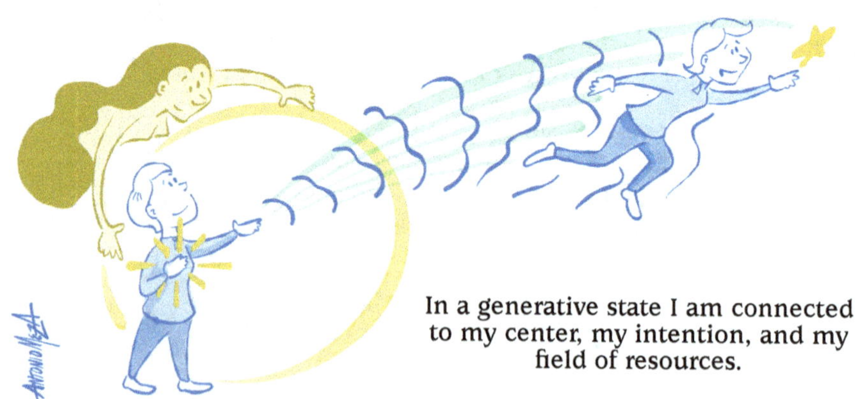

In a generative state I am connected to my center, my intention, and my field of resources.

The Importance of a Generative State

A fundamental premise of Generative Coaching is that, in order to create generative outcomes and solutions, we need to bring our filters into a generative state – our somatic filters, our cognitive filters and our field filters. This allows us to reach out into what we call the quantum field of possibilities and explore: "What is possible? What are some new possibilities that we can actually bring into expression now?" The generative state then allows us to transform those "possibilities" into "actualities" by putting them into concrete expressions. This is the essence of Generative Coaching.

Given the significance that a generative state plays in Generative Coaching, one question that we are frequently asked is, "Is every person capable of being generative?" Our answer, of course, is "Yes." We do believe everybody has that capability. In fact, we can say that in many ways we are born generative. If you have ever spent time around a newborn baby, you know that everything is new to them. They are experiencing and learning everything for the first time. So, it seems clear that we are born in a generative state. However, what happens is that, from the time we are born, we also begin to get "programmed." We learn routines. We learn to think and act in particular ways. So our cognitive and somatic filters become more fixed. Similarly, we learn to fit into our family, into our society, into our culture, and our field filters become more set. Consequently, our level of generativity begins to proportionately diminish.

We are born in a generative state and, as we grow older, our cognitive and somatic filters become more fixed. Our level of generativity begins to diminish.

As an illustration, there was a very interesting study that was done in which people at different stages in life were observed with regard to the amount and quality of their movements. The observers had a way of mapping different movements of the hands, the head, the posture, the body, etc. What they noticed with newborns and very young babies was that if they observed them for one hour, they would see about a thousand different unique movements. If they observed older children, such as ten-year-olds, they no longer saw a thousand different unique movements, but rather several hundred. If they observed people who were in their thirties for an hour, they might be lucky to see a hundred movements. In older people, they might see half of that. The implication was that the amount of generativity and diversity of somatic expression tends to diminish as people get older. Of course, in some ways, the reason for that is that we become more optimized. We are wasting less time and less energy. But the other side of that is that we start losing the capacity for flexibility and generativity.

This example relates to our somatic filters. We can see something similar with the cognitive mind. Children or younger people, in general, have a lot of new ideas. As people get older, they tend to recycle the same ideas. Again, there are positives with that because, as we like to point out, not everything requires generativity. Stability is important

too. Such "programming" helps us to optimize what we are doing and thinking. That is also necessary for our success and survival. In fact, managing this complementarity between stability and change, the familiar and the new, optimization and flexibility, etc., is one of the key issues we deal with in generative change.

So, while everybody has the capacity to be generative, there is a natural tendency to become more and more fixed in our patterns. This is one of the reasons that the notion of practice is so important in generative change and generative coaching. We all know that to keep flexibility in our bodies, we need to practice. We need to do some kind of physical exercise such as stretching, yoga or other kinds of movements to keep the body supple. Robert's wife Deborah, for example, teaches a practice called The Five Rhythms, created by Gabrielle Roth. One of the values of this practice is that you get to move your body in different ways.

So, by practicing, we maintain not only mobility, but we can increase our capacity for flexibility and generativity. It is just like anything else, such as riding a bicycle or playing a musical instrument. The more you practice, the more that potential is there for you. So, the idea of a generative practice is a kind of paradox. It is something you do repetitively in order to keep opening more creative possibilities.

Engaging Multiple Intelligences

Another key to being generative is to activate and apply multiple intelligences—verbal, visual, somatic, emotional, metaphorical, etc. To be generative, it is necessary to go beyond the verbal cognitive intellect. When clients are defining their direction and intention for change, for instance, in addition to requesting a verbal description of the desired state, we will also ask for a visual image. "What is your mental picture for that desired state? What image do you see?" Verbal representations come more from the "left-brain" and focus more on objects and sequencing while visual representations are generated by the "right-brain" and emphasize patterns and relationships. Incorporating color into the images can bring out a whole different level of dynamics

One of the other essential areas of intelligence necessary to promote generative change is the intelligence of the body; our "somatic intelligence." In generative coaching, for every key piece of cognitive information we gather, we will also get a somatic model. We will ask, "What is a movement or gesture that expresses that?" For instance, we will say, "Show your desired state with your body." This often brings greater insight into what is going on than a lot of verbalization. Somatic representations tend to more effectively capture the relational and emotional dimensions related to a situation than words.

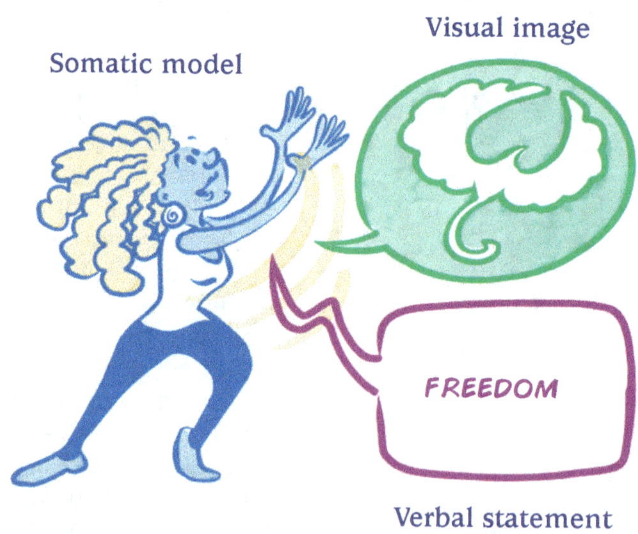

The Role of Aesthetic Intelligence in Generative Coaching

Aesthetic intelligence is another key to being sustainably generative. It is all about how things relate to each other. Aesthetic intelligence is the basis of harmony, beauty, and balance. It involves sensitivity to how different parts of something (such as music, painting, food, architecture, dance, life, etc.) relate to one another and to the larger whole. What this means with respect to the generative coaching process is welcoming and making space for all parts of the change process.

If a client feels anxious, for instance, we avoid saying, "Don't be anxious. You shouldn't be anxious." In this changing, dangerous world today, it would be crazy not to be anxious, not to be afraid, not to be worried, not to be, in some cases, depressed or bored. The questions related to aesthetic intelligence are, "What is the complement to this anxiety? What resources can we bring to balance it?" If you are too anxious, you become obsessive-compulsive. If you have no concern, you can do things that will make your situation worse for yourself and others. So, the question of aesthetic intelligence is always, "What is the right balance?"

Stephen likes to use the metaphor of cooking. He says, "A little bit of this and a little bit of that." So, if you have too much salt, it tastes bad. If there is no salt, something is missing. This is how a Generative Coach looks at a client. We view each person as complex system of different parts. To be generative, these parts have to be in the right relationship to each other. This is why we say that the optimum is not always the maximum. For example, the optimum amount of energy is not always the maximum amount of energy.

In *Generative Coaching Volume 2*, for instance, Stephen introduced the key notion of "archetypal energies" such as fierceness, force, strength; tenderness, softness, openness; playfulness, lightness, and joyfulness. The question in any given situation is, "What is the right level and combination of those energies?" That is what we are calling aesthetic intelligence. This is one of the reasons we frequently use scaling in generative coaching sessions. We invite our clients to rate their experience of something on a scale of zero to ten. We want to help our clients develop "volume controls." Sometimes we are turning down the fierceness and turning up the playfulness. Other times we decrease both the fierceness and playfulness and increase the tenderness and softness. We do not want to simply turn one off and one on. It is important to keep some amount of each of them present. This is why we are always first welcoming what is there and then asking, "What is the right relationship between all of these things?"

In fact, it is our view that the lack of aesthetic intelligence is responsible for many of the obstacles that our clients experience when they are attempting to reach their desired states. Imposed change or attempts to make change often disrupt the balance that has stabilized the present state (even if it is not optimal) and the "obstacle" is emerging in an attempt to regain that balance.

As an example, let's say a person needs to spend more time with an aging parent and wants to create more of a sense of connection, openness and softness with that parent. However, as they do this and have less time for themselves, they begin to experience a desire to put up stronger emotional and temporal boundaries with respect to that parent. This can bring up a sense of guilt and lead to an inner conflict about wanting to spend time with their parent. If the person tries to suppress their desire for boundaries and supplant it with openness and softness, that desire for boundaries can start to show up in uncomfortable and distorted ways, such as unintentional exasperation with the parent if he or she needs extra assistance. This is the opposite of the openness and softness the person wants to create. In this form, it appears as a problem or an obstacle to reaching their desired state.

In fact, the antithesis of a generative state is what we call a *CRASH* State: *Contracted*, *Reactive*, caught in *Analysis* paralysis, *Separated* from ourselves and our resources and *Hostile* towards ourselves and others. This leads to the opposite of aesthetic intelligence and instead creates the experience of what we call "neuromuscular lock" in which our inner maps and possible responses become fixed and rigid. When our attempts to create balance are dealt with and expressed through a *CRASH* State they show up as symptoms and obstacles.

Contracted

Reactive

Analysis Paralysis

Separated

Hostile/ Hurting/ Hating

The CRASH state is disconnected from the Whole

Working Creatively with Obstacles to Generativity

One of the unique features of generative coaching and generative change is our approach to working with such obstacles. Rather than seeing them as a problem, we see obstacles as a necessary and vital part of creative change. They are the signal that something is out of balance in the client's system or "holon." Key to transforming that obstacle is first welcoming it and making a place for it, and then finding the root cause of what is creating and maintaining the imbalance.

As an example, usually the reason that people question whether everyone can be generative is because we all have met individuals who do not seem to be very generative at all. Instead, they are entrenched in a particular way of being that creates ongoing problems for themselves and the others whose lives they affect. Even if they say that they want to change, they keep reverting to the patterns that escalate their problems. Core questions for a generative coach would be, "What is the obstacle that is preventing this person from being generative? How can we transform that obstacle into a resource?"

A common cause for such obstacles is having a limiting belief. As I pointed out at the beginning of this chapter, one of the things we will be working with in this volume is the phenomenon of beliefs. Some of our beliefs empower us and promote generativity. Others create what we call "belief barriers" that prevent us from achieving our desired states.

Belief Barriers

A good example of addressing such obstacles in generative change work would be that of a client who does not want to do somatic movements when asked to by the coach. This would clearly initially show up as a potential problem to moving forward with the coaching session. As a generative coach, we would immediately say, "Welcome" to that resistance. We would follow by saying, "You do not want to make the somatic movements. That is interesting. I am sure it makes sense. Something there is needing to be heard or held or healed. Welcome." We are going to really want to make a lot of space for that resistance. We would then say to the client, "Let us explore what is it that makes you so resistant to wanting to make a somatic movement." We might even ask the client, "Can you show me with your body what your resistance to doing the somatic movement is like?" Of course, whatever happens next, we are going to say, "Welcome."

Oftentimes, such resistance is going to be related to a belief. Motivational issues are almost always related to beliefs and values. So, the question becomes, "What is the belief that is creating that resistance?" Perhaps it is a belief like, "I will appear awkward and foolish" or "I am afraid I will lose control." Then, as we will see in the coming chapters, we will look for what positive intention drives the belief. We will also look for complementary resources that can satisfy that intention in such a way that the client can regain some type of harmony and balance.

The Six Steps of Generative Coaching

The issues and principles described so far in this chapter are what the six steps of generative coaching are designed to address. As with the previous two volumes of Generative Coaching, this book is organized around the six fundamental steps of generative coaching. These steps walk us through all of the stages required to produce generative change.

1. Opening a COACH Field.

This field is created by the resonance between the coach and client when they are both *Centered*, *Open*, *Aware*, *Connected* to their resources and to each other, and *Holding* what is happening between them from a state of curiosity and resourcefulness. In this state, the "channel is open" and the movement between the quantum world of possibilities and the concrete world of ongoing classical reality flows easily.

Open a COACH field

2. Establishing a Positive Intention

At this step we want to find out, "What do you want to create in your life? What is the generative goal? What do you want more of (and less of)?" And we engage multiple intelligences (words, images and somatic models) to represent that intention.

Set a positive intention/direction

3. Developing a Generative Performance State

This involves bringing in the resources that are needed in order for the client to be able to go towards his or her desired state. These resources come from both within the client and also from his or her larger "field" of resources.

Develop a generative
(creative) state

Take action

4. Moving Into Action

At this stage, we begin to explore, "What are the concrete steps that need to be taken in order to reach the desired state?"

5. Transforming Obstacles

When we move into action, right on cue, come the obstacles. We need to meet those obstacles and creatively find a way to transform them. As always, we are trying to turn these obstacles into opportunities.

Transform obstacles/resistances

6. Practices for Sustaining and Deepening the Changes

As we pointed out earlier, practices help us to develop the necessary capacity for both focus and flexibility necessary to achieve and maintain our desired states.

Establish practices for continued creativity

Doing Generative Coaching Online

One challenge for coaches in today's world has been a major shift to more online as opposed to in-person coaching. We are frequently asked, "How exactly should I perform online Generative Coaching sessions? What is important while performing an online session? What focus of attention is really important?"

Whether we are doing a Generative Coaching session in person or online, the six steps are always going to be our guide. When working virtually, however, it is particularly important to keep access to the somatic mind. One of the biggest challenges of doing things online is that it is easy for people to just come up into their head and just have this purely verbal, cognitive interaction. With today's technology, in an online session you can hear the person and you can see the person. Obviously, one of the big barriers is being unable to touch the person. So, this is an area where we have to be generative and find other possibilities. When we are working online, it becomes even more significant that we keep access to movement and to the body. Rather than sit in front of the screen, for instance, we will stand up and ask clients to join us in standing and moving. And we find mirroring their somatic movements to be especially important.

Santa Cruz, California 9AM

Generative fields are created through resonance, involving multiple intelligences.

Another challenge of an online session relates to what we call the "field." People wonder, "How do you create the generative field between the coach and client in a virtual interaction?" There is a tendency to think of that field as being easier to create when you are physically together with another person. We know, for example, that there is what is called the "human bioenergetic field" that can be enhanced by physical proximity.

It is important to keep in mind, however, that field effects are not necessarily limited by time and space. This is true of every type of field including physical fields. What we are calling a generative field is created by resonance. It is like a type of "quantum entanglement." When there is sufficient resonance (especially resonance involving multiple intelligences), a generative field can be created even with people on the other side of the planet and who are speaking a different language. In fact, all of the coaching demonstrations we will be presenting in this book were done online and through an interpreter with people on different continents.

In summary, when giving a Generative Coaching session online, (1) we will still follow the same six steps; (2), we want to be giving special attention to keeping the somatic mind active in ourselves and our clients; and (3) we want to seek resonance with our clients (in the head, the heart, the gut, the body, etc.) in order to build the proper quality of a generative field. In the coming chapters we will provide a number of demonstrations of how to do this.

For Presence

Awaken to the mystery of being here

and enter the quiet immensity of your own presence.

Have joy and peace in the temple of your senses.

Receive encouragement when new frontiers beckon.

Respond to the call of your gift and the courage to follow its path.

Let the flame of anger free you of all falsity.

May warmth of heart keep your presence aflame.

May anxiety never linger about you.

May your outer dignity mirror an inner dignity of soul.

Take time to celebrate the quiet miracles that seek no attention.

Be consoled by the secret symmetry of your soul.

May you experience each day as a sacred gift woven around the heart of wonder.

John O'Donohue
(from **Benedictus**)

Chapter 2

Step 1
Opening the COACH Field

Entering a COACH State and establishing a COACH field is the foundation of all generative change work. This is because it creates a container that makes it possible to hold all of the dimensions of the change process—present state, desired state, resources, action plans, obstacles, etc., in such a way that we can apply aesthetic intelligence to find harmonious and sustainable solutions.

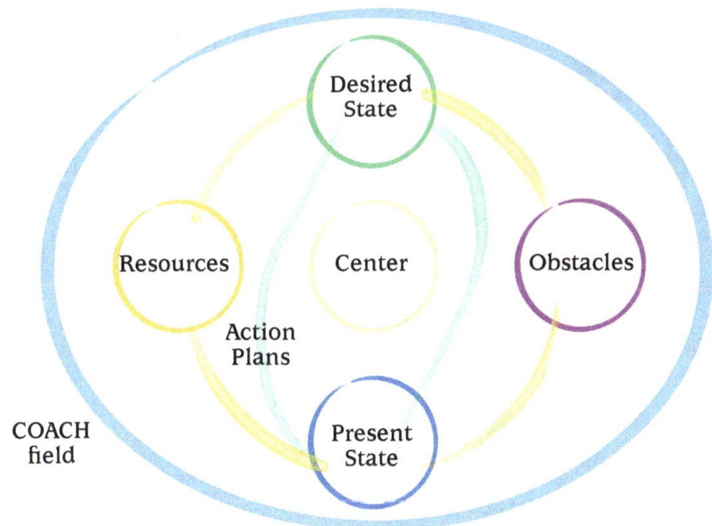

The COACH field creates a container that makes it possible to hold all of the dimensions of the change process and find harmonious and sustainable solutions

The ability to create and maintain a strong COACH field throughout the coaching session is essential for generative coaching. Without it there is no possibility for generativity. That is why it is important to have multiple ways of engaging (and re-engaging) a robust COACH State. In the previous two volumes, we have presented four basic methods for doing this: (1) revivifying COACH-like experiences; (2) guided process of C-O-A-C-H; (3) the three mindfulness drops; and (4) the three-point attention technique. In this chapter, we will present some other ways we can lead clients into a COACH State and deepen it further.

Active Centering

There is a tendency for people to view the COACH State as a type of passive, meditation-like experience that is mostly associated with positive feelings. While that can be one expression of the COACH State, it is much more than that. The qualities of the COACH State—Centered, Open, Alert and Connected to resources, then Holding what is happening from a state of curiosity and resourcefulness—can be present even during the most intense physical or emotional exertion. In fact, this is precisely the state that high performing athletes are constantly seeking and practicing.

Centered

Open

Aware

Connected

Holding

The COACH State

What we call "Active Centering" is a way to help clients dynamically learn and develop the key qualities of the COACH State. It can be particularly useful when doing virtual coaching sessions because the process emphasizes engaging the body and our somatic filters. The following is a transcript of actively leading a client into a COACH State. Of course, the coach is not only giving the instructions but also demonstrating the movements, which serves to help build the COACH field.

One of the first things I'm going to invite us to do is a couple of things that help to really get grounded and centered somatically. One of the first things to do is to take your right hand and your right leg and cross them over your left hand and leg. After you do that, you want to find your balance. Then you're going to do that the other way—crossing your left hand and leg over your right side. Do this three times each way. You're crossing right to left and then left to right.

Get grounded

Somatic centering

To bring a little bit more energy and balance, one of the other things you can do is take your right elbow and touch your left knee, then the left elbow to the right knee. Do that three times each direction. The only way to make this movement is around the physical center of your body.

Another thing that will really test how centered you are is to balance on one leg. You lift one of your legs and find your balance. When you think you have a good balance, you bring your hands together in front of you, still balancing on that one leg. If you think you really have a good balance, then you close your eyes and notice if you can keep that balance with your eyes closed. Then go to the other leg and do the same thing. First, find your balance. When you have it, bring the hands closer together. Then, try closing your eyes. Do that three times on each foot. It should get a little easier each time. One hint is to keep your knees flexible. Don't stiffen your leg. Another helpful thing is to remember to breathe, of course. Do that now the third time on one leg then, onto the other leg. Find the balance. Then just stand on both of your feet and you should feel much more centered and balanced.

Find the balance

Open your vertical channel

Once we are grounded and centered, we want to open the vertical channel. To do that, you want to put your fingers around your thumbs to make a fist and then put your hands down by your side. Then, push your fists down, bend your knees and breathe in like you are pushing down into the earth. As you breathe out, raise your hands open and high over your head. Go up on the toes and find your balance. Do that three times, breathing in and pushing down, then breathing out reaching up, and lengthen your spine.

COACH State Tai Chi

One of our favorite methods of opening a COACH field with a client is a form of active centering that I call the "COACH State Tai Chi." Tai Chi movements, as we know, are made very consciously and slowly. The following is a transcript of guiding a client through five movements associated with each aspect of the COACH State. Again, the coach not only gives the instructions but demonstrates the movements to create somatic resonance with the client.

We start with the movement where we take our hands, bring them next to each other in front of us and we are pushing down. This is where we are centering—bending the knees and pushing the hands down in front of us.

From there, we slowly we open our arms out wide in front of us, like they are opening out from the heart center.

Then, we bring the arms above the head and make a gesture of expanding awareness.

Then, we start to connect. We want to bring the hands together and slowly touch our head, our heart, our belly and our legs. And, as we do, we are connecting to all of the resources—intellectual, emotional, intuitive and somatic. We can also feel the connection of our feet to the earth.

Then, we can put our arms out in front of us in a gesture of holding. As we make each gesture again, we can say to ourselves silently, "I'm centered, I'm open, I'm alert, aware and awake, I'm connected, and I'm ready to hold whatever is happening." So, centered, open, alert, connected, and ready.

We find this simple sequence of movements a very powerful way to introduce clients to the COACH State, and also to quickly return to a COACH State if needed later in the session. Of course, it is possible to do these COACH State Tai Chi movements sitting as well. What is important is to continually take that time to remind ourselves to reconnect to these qualities that form the foundation of a generative state and a generative field.

Finding Your Center

Maintaining the COACH State in the face of problems and obstacles is one of the most crucial and most challenging aspects of generative change. When things become difficult, chaotic or confusing, it is so easy to CRASH. In order to really deepen the capability to stay in COACH State, one of the things that I am often doing with my clients is an exercise I call "Finding Your Center." It is a process for developing self-awareness that involves looking at different reference experiences for being centered and creating a strong anchor for what is common to them. The basic steps are:

1. Find (or if necessary, imagine) three examples of activities in which you fully felt a sense of flow and being yourself.

2. Find some examples of challenging times in which you were able to stay centered and resourceful.

3. Identify the common internal qualities shared by all these experiences, in particular with respect to feelings. How do you know when you are connected to your center?

4. Use this to establish and anchor a felt sense of your "center."

So, we are going to be looking for three examples of a very strong sense of being centered and of being in a creative state of flow we could say, then some other examples of what you might call "resilience"— of being able to come back to a COACH State under very challenging circumstances. This is going to give us a foundation for creating a strong anchor for being centered.

As always, when we do generative coaching, we are not trying to rigidly follow a technique. Our generative coaching prototypes are intended to provide guidelines that can be adapted to different situations and clients.

Demonstration of Finding your Center

The following is a transcript of a demonstration that Robert did as part of a virtual training course.

Robert: *Welcome! This is our first virtual demonstration, and I can see that it looks like you are already standing.*

Kate: *Yes.*

Robert: *So, I am going to join you [stands.] So, I want to do some exploration on how to create an even deeper COACH State for you. Before we begin, let us even just take a moment and see if we can come out of just this virtual world to feel that sense of our presence and our connection together right now. [Both take a breath.] Yeah, I feel that too.*

And Kate, as we are getting ready to get started, and as we think about the importance of a COACH State, I am curious about what kind of intention that you have for this time and especially for this session. Is there something that would really be useful for you?

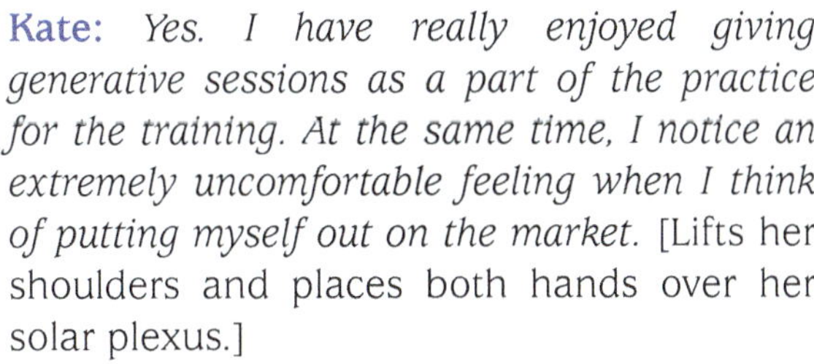

Kate: *Yes. I have really enjoyed giving generative sessions as a part of the practice for the training. At the same time, I notice an extremely uncomfortable feeling when I think of putting myself out on the market. [Lifts her shoulders and places both hands over her solar plexus.]*

Robert: *[Mirrors the posture and gesture.] I can see there is already a somatic model for that uncomfortable feeling. Let us say, "Welcome." I am sure that makes a lot of sense. There is something there that is really wanting to be held, to be heard, maybe to be healed. Let us breathe with that [silence].*

And we want to have a very strong sense of your center so that you can, first of all, create a place for uncomfortable feelings and then also bring resources to it.

So Kate, what I would like to ask you to do first is, let us explore some situations where you do not have this reaction, you have the opposite —where you really feel, "I am strong and confident." What would be a situation where yet you feel completely calm, confident and creative?

Kate: *Anything connected to travel. Even if any obstacles come around, I feel brave.*

Robert: *Great. So let us start there. Let us find an experience where you were traveling and you were just feeling "I am in my flow. This is easy for me." Really put yourself there and see what you are seeing, hear what you are hearing and especially feel what you are feeling. Bring even more awareness to what is happening inside of you and how you experience the sense of your center in that situation. What would be your somatic model?*

Kate: [Extends her arms out in front of her and slowly brings them to her belly.]

Robert: [Mirrors the gesture.] *Yeah. I like that. Great. So that is finding really a way to bring that attention to that place of centeredness. And on a scale of zero to ten, how strongly would you feel that you are centered in that?*

Kate: *Between eight and nine.*

Robert: *Wonderful. So, what I would like to do now is to find another situation. This first reference experience was about traveling. What is another situation where you feel really confident, grounded and centered.*

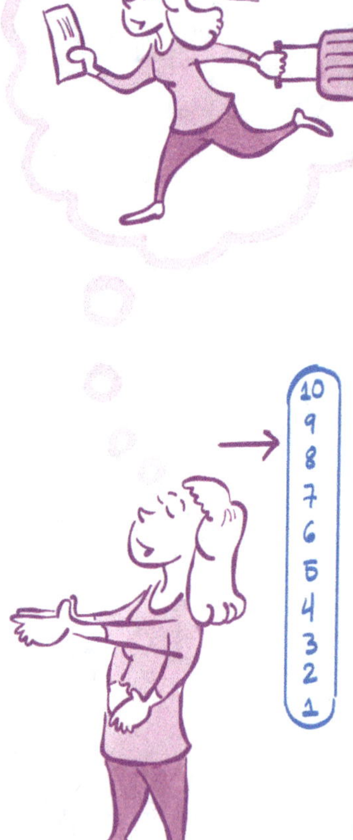

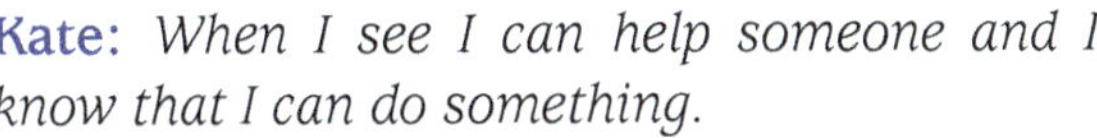

Kate: *When I see I can help someone and I know that I can do something.*

Robert: *Let us go into that experience when you see that you can help someone, and you know you can do something. Let us take the time to breathe that through. Pick a particular example and remember seeing what you saw, hearing what you heard, bringing an even deeper awareness to what happens especially inside of you. And what would be your movement for that?*

Kate: [Makes a repetitive gesture with her hands, moving them outward from her body and then back towards her body.] *It is a kind of exchange. I know that when I can achieve that, I will receive back as much happiness by knowing that I succeeded.*

Robert: [Mirrors the gesture.] *That is great.*

So now Kate, if you reflect on both of those experiences—travel [extends arms out in front and slowly brings them to the belly] *and seeing you can help* [moves hands outward from the body and then back towards the body]*—what is the same? There are differences between them but what is the same for you about both of them?*

Kate: *Somatically or from a feeling?*

Robert: *Both or either.*

Kate: [Repeats the gestures associated with both experiences.] *In both situations, from the first moment on, I anticipate that I will succeed. Even if I feel a little bit overwhelmed at some point, I am centered and I believe that I will succeed* [smiles broadly.]

Robert: *So, I want to say to that, "Welcome!" I really see that there is something in you that comes so much more alive in that.*

Let us do one more exploration. We have travel and when you see that you can help somebody. What is another situation where you have that sense of deep centered confidence in yourself?

Kate: [Pauses then breathes deeply.] *I would say, once I am doing one these generative coaching sessions, I feel this kind of peace in my mind. Once it is started, there is no way back, nothing can go wrong and what I can do is just step forward and step forward.*

Robert: *So, put yourself into that situation where you have already started a coaching session. See what you see, hear what you hear and feel what you are feeling. What is your somatic model?*

Kate: [Brings her hands up to her head and then slowly moves them downward in front of her body.] *There is this kind of peace of mind, and clarity.*

Robert: [Mirrors the gesture.] *Peace of mind and clarity.*

So now, let us put all three of these together. You have travel [extends arms out in front and slowly brings them to the belly], *seeing you can help* [moves hands outward from the body and then back towards the body] *and you have that peace of mind once you have started a coaching session* [brings hands up to the head and then slowly moves them downward in front of the body]. *What is common to all three of these experiences?*

Kate: [Slowly and intently makes the three gestures.] *It feels like staying true to myself. That to be in a COACH state at all, I have to take care of myself first.*

Robert: *When you say that, a big breath certainly came into my body and to me. It feels quite profound.*

As a final exploration, I would like to invite you to think of times when you are able to stay centered even though things were really challenging. Even though it was difficult you were still able to come back to your center and stay in the center. I am curious if you have any experiences of that that you could share.

Kate: *Yes, for example, there was one time where I was traveling from Germany to Russia—I have Russian citizenship, but I live in Germany—and I mixed up the dates and this was the last day of my visa. And I was just about to go through the passport control and the officer tells me, "Are you planning to come back? Because it is your last day." And I had twenty minutes while queueing for my flight to decide, do I fly, or do I not fly? And I decided to fly. It was a quite intense experience because I was going for just three days.*

Robert: *Wow! That sounds like a really good one because that is a big challenge. So, take a moment and put yourself back into that situation. And, as you relive it, notice anything that you are aware of that allows you to keep coming back to your center. See what you see, hear what you hear and feel what you feel.*

Kate: *Something deep inside of me strongly believes that everything will be fine.*

Robert: *When you say deep inside of you, is there a particular place in your body? What would be your somatic model for that?*

Kate: *It starts in my heart* [touches the upper center of her chest with both hands] *and it kind of goes down into the ground to the very center of the earth* [moves her hands down her torso to her legs].

Robert: [Mirrors the gesture.] *A deep belief that everything will be fine.*

So, now let's put all of these reference experiences together. There is the travel [extends arms out in front and slowly brings them to the belly] *and seeing you can help* [moves hands outward from the body and then back towards the body]. *There is that anticipation that, even if you feel a little overwhelmed, you know you will succeed. Then we add to that the peace of mind once you have started a coaching session* [brings hands up to the head and then slowly moves them downward in front of the body] *and the feeling of staying true to yourself and taking care of yourself first. Next, we bring in that decision to fly and the deep belief that everything will be fine* [touches the upper center of the chest with both hands and moves them down the torso to the legs].

Kate: [Repeatedly makes the four gestures in a slow rhythmic motion.]

Robert: *And then think of putting yourself out on the market as a generative coach. What do you experience? Do you feel ready to do that?*

Kate: [Slowly and intently makes the four gestures then smiles broadly.] *Yes! It does not feel like a problem at all anymore. In fact, it feels like I am stepping forward into my place on this Earth and that this is what I have been put here to bring to others.*

Robert: *Fantastic! I send you my full support for that.*

Now let's find an anchor for this new resource. What can help you stay connected to this deeply centered place?

Kate: *What comes to my mind is to really keep a connection to these somatic models. I think they will really help me and remind me that, even in difficult situations, I am able to stay centered.*

Robert: *Great. I think, the somatic anchors are so useful. It is often also nice to have an external anchor to remind you, which could be a picture, even taking a selfie of yourself in that posture of connection to the center of the earth. A picture of the earth could be another possible anchor. And then you can put it in your office or somewhere where, even if you do not consciously think about it or try to remember it, it is always there to remind you of this deep belief that everything will be fine.*

Kate: *Yes. I will do that. Thank you.*

Robert: *It has been my pleasure.*

And now that we have ended the coaching part of this session, especially since we are in this new virtual medium, it would be good to get some feedback from you about what you found to be the most helpful or useful.

Kate: *Well, as much as I would love to be next to you physically now to be able to embrace you and say how much this meant to me, for me, once you create this generative field, it doesn't matter. I do not feel any barrier to do the generative sessions or our training online.*

Robert: *Thank you. I have also enjoyed a lovely quality of connection.*

Breakdown of the Finding Your Center Process

The purpose of this process is to create a deeper felt sense of connection to our center, which is the cornerstone of the COACH state. Without a strong connection to our center, the rest of the COACH qualities will be compromised. Our center is not simply a physical location in the body. It is a "source" that produces all of our resources. In fact, the term "re-source" is revealing. Even though the content of our resources may vary tremendously (i.e., focus, flexibility, calmness, determination, playfulness, etc.) they all share a common denominator or source —our center. And the deeper connection we have to our center, the more profound the resources will be that are available to us.

We can see this in the demonstration with Kate. As she deepened her connection to her center, her resources went from "feeling brave" to "knowing she could succeed even if she felt a bit overwhelmed, to "peace of mind and clarity" to "staying true to herself and taking care of herself first," to "a deep belief that everything will be fine that went down to the center of the earth" to "stepping forward into her place on this earth to do what she had been put here for." This path of resources begins at the level of capabilities and moves through a series of empowering beliefs that lead to a sense of identity and mission.

Opening and deepening a COACH field, especially if it is being done through a virtual medium like the demonstration with Kate, requires that we ourselves as coaches be deeply centered, open, aware and connected. When doing this process, it is important to make sure that we are present and can really feel that sense of connection with our partner. If we are working virtually, that sense of connection comes through the screen: not "on" the screen but through the screen.

That part is not about technique, but our own presence, centering in ourselves, and really feeling that sense of connection with our partner.

We often begin, as shown in the demonstration with Kate, by asking the coachee where it would be useful and important for them to have a stronger COACH state. In Kate's case, it was that when she thought about getting ready to "put herself out there" as a generative coach and encountered "an extremely uncomfortable feeling." Naturally, we are going to welcome the presence of this feeling as a key member of the team or "holon." In fact, one of the main purposes of this process is to be able to be with uncomfortable feelings from a more resourceful place, rather than trying to fight it, repress it or give in to it.

Our first step is having the coachee find some reference experiences for being deeply centered and resourceful. We invite the coachee to fully re-experience it—not just think about it—but to relive it. In the demo with Kate, Robert kept using the words, "see what you saw, hear what you heard and feel what you felt." It is also important to give the coachee time to access the experience and bring even more awareness to the inner "differences that make the difference." Finding the somatic model of that inner state is an important way to facilitate that. As generative coaches, we also want to join our coachees in their experience as a way to strengthen our field connection with them.

When you have explored two such resourceful reference experiences, the next step is to discover what is common to them. Even though the outer contexts and inner experience may be quite different, what do they share? Where to they overlap? This invariably takes you to a deeper level, closer to the source. In Kate's case, there was feeling brave with respect to traveling and then there was the knowing she could do something to help somebody. What the two shared was the belief that she would succeed, even if she felt a bit overwhelmed at first.

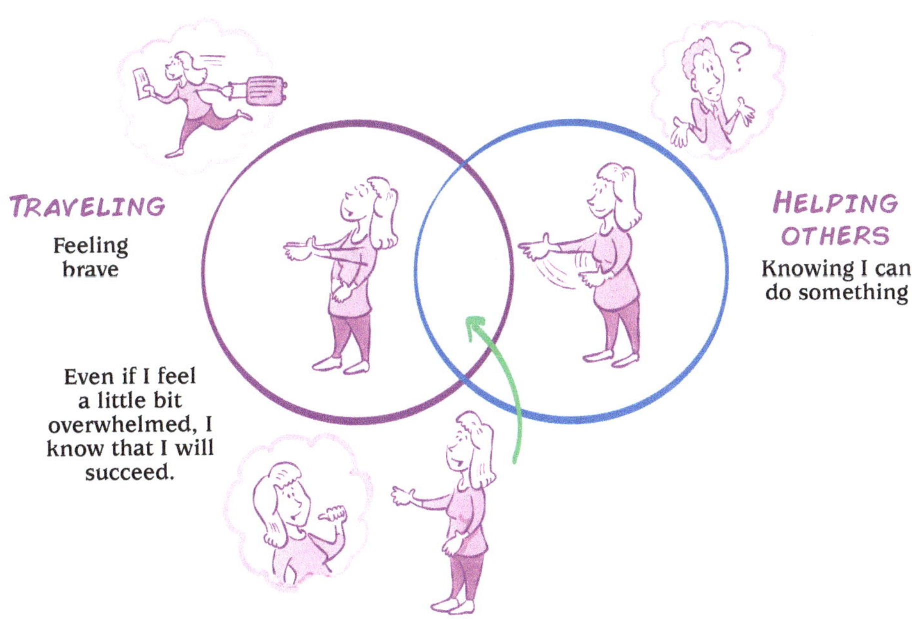

Finding a third positive reference experience and looking for how it overlaps the others will take you even deeper. Reviewing the somatic models for each of the experiences is very helpful in doing this. Frequently, there will be some obvious gesture or quality of movement that shows up in each of the somatic models. Exploring that common gesture or movement can bring deep insights.

In Kate's case, adding the reference experience of the peace of mind and clarity that came with starting a coaching session to her other two resourceful situations brought out the common factor of "staying true to herself and taking care of herself first." This begins to touch on the level of identity.

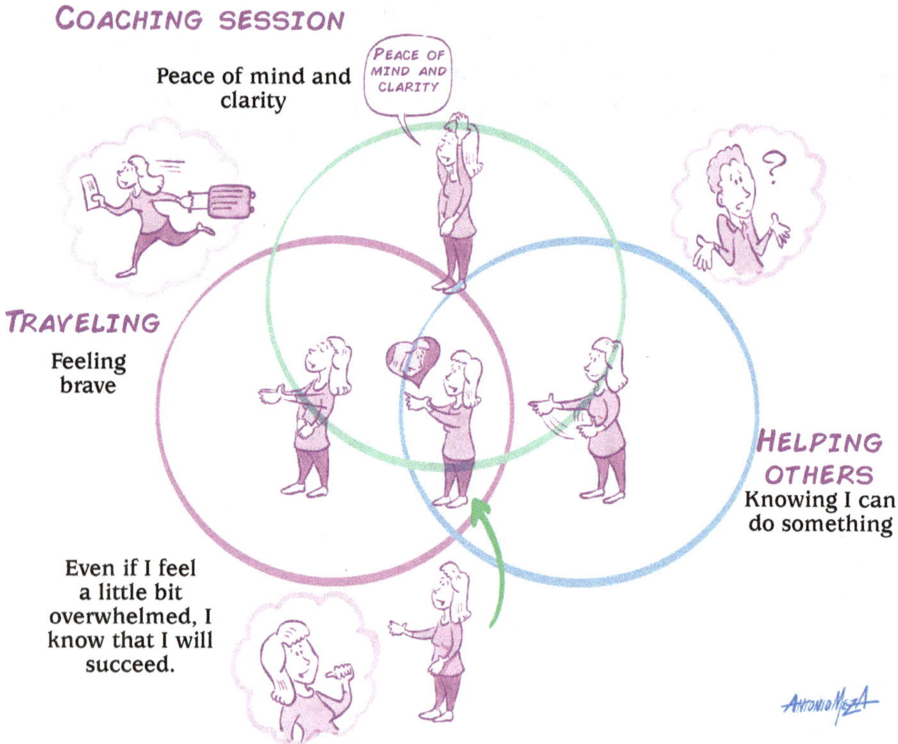

Another step that can help to get an even stronger sense of centering, to have the coachee think of very challenging situations where he or she was still able to stay centered, resilient and resourceful. In the example with Kate, this was the "strong belief that everything will be fine" associated with her decision to fly, even though her visa had expired. Finding the overlap of this experience with the others took her to the even deeper sense of "stepping forward into her place on this Earth to do what she had been put here for."

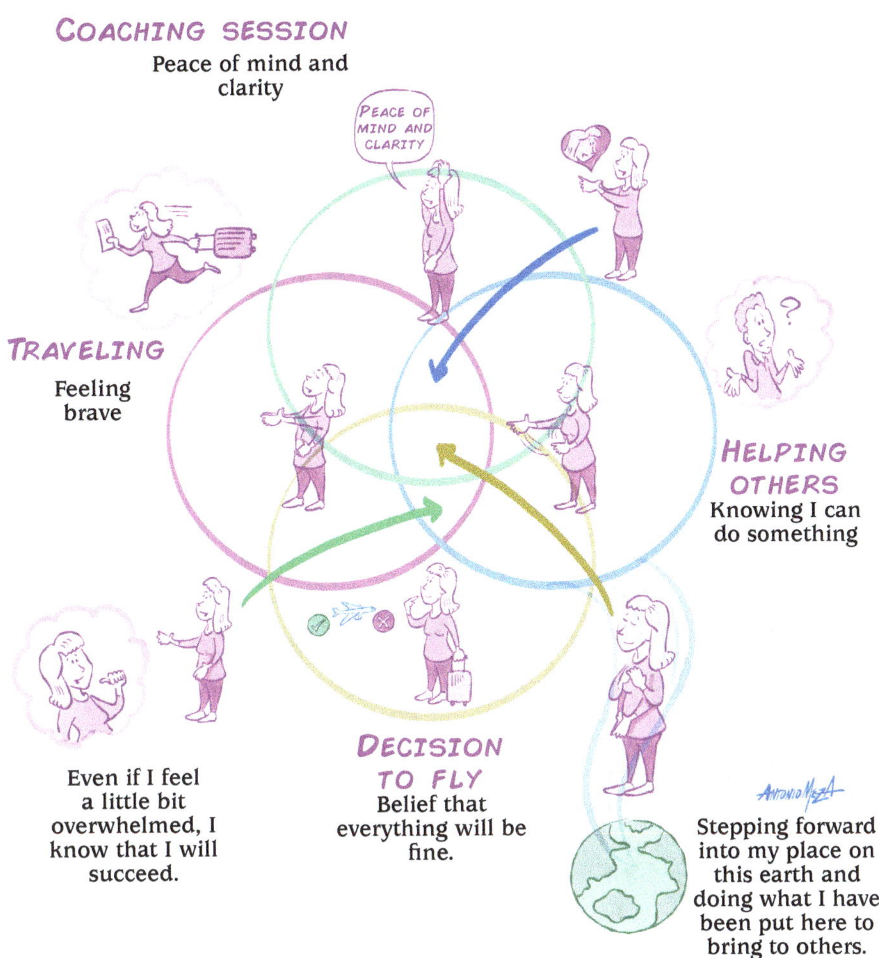

By this time, the coachee will have developed a very powerful and profound COACH state and you can revisit the challenging situation that was identified at the start of the session. You can use the somatic models as anchors to facilitate that process. It can also be helpful to find and external anchor (an object, picture, piece of clothing, photograph, etc.) to use as a reminder of the experience of being in a deeply centered COACH state. As we saw in the demonstration with Kate, whatever aspect of our experience that we can hold within a COACH state, is not going to be perceived as a problem. And it will most likely be profoundly transformed.

We believe that this is one of the most powerful and important things that we can do in this time in our lives, and in the world—keep coming back to COACH state and holding whatever is there from a robust COACH state. This is the foundation for how we create a better life and a better world.

Our deepest fear is not that we are inadequate. Our fear is that we are powerful beyond measure. It is our light, not our darkness, that frightens us. We ask ourselves:"Who am I to be brilliant, gorgeous, talented, fabulous?"

Actually, who are you not to be? You are a child of God. Your playing small does not serve the world. There is nothing enlightened about shrinking, so that other people won't feel insecure around you.

We are all meant to shine, as children do. We are born to make manifest the glory of God that is within us. It is not in some of us; it is in everyone. As we make our own light shine, we unconsciously give others permission to do the same. As we are liberated from our fear, our presence automatically liberates others.

—Marianne Williamson

Chapter 3

Step 2
Setting Intentions/Goals

The second step of the *Generative Coaching process* is setting a goal or an intention. This can be particularly challenging when the context that we are in is changing and uncertain. We wonder, "How am I supposed to know what I want to do when there is so much potential uncertainty?" This is where the value of what we are calling an "intention" comes in. An intention defines a direction in which we will be moving rather than detail a specific result.

In situations involving high levels of change or uncertainty, we cannot know or be too specific about the exact steps we will take or the precise destination we will ultimately arrive at. The environment is changing, i.e., "where" and "when" things are happening. And our behaviors (i.e., "what" we are doing) are changing in response to that. Our capabilities also have to change—"How am I going to do it?" We have to develop completely new capabilities. This means that we must turn to deeper levels—like our values, our identity, and our sense of purpose or mission—to be our guides in these times of uncertainty.

Our basic question in **Step 2** is, "What do you most want to create in this world?" Or, "What do you most want to become in this world?" Especially in uncertain times, people are likely to say, "I don't know! I don't know what's possible." One of the frames that I sometimes suggest to my clients to reflect on in such contexts is not so much related to "what do you want to create" as "what will you regret if you don't?"

The Top Five Regrets of the Dying

As a starting point, we will share with them the *"five lessons"* from dying people from a book that was written some years ago by a woman named Bronnie, an Australian nurse. She spent several years working in palliative care, caring for patients in the last twelve weeks of their lives. In her book *The Top Five Regrets of the Dying*, she recorded her conversations with people about any regrets they had or what they would do differently in their lives. Most had not honored even half of their dreams. They went to their death realizing that this was a choice they had made, and they deeply regretted having never really lived their dreams, or even part of them. As Irish playwright George Bernard Shaw said, "Most people go their graves with their music still in them." These five regrets can give us some very interesting guidance when we think about setting intentions.

The first and most common regret was, "I wish I'd had the courage to live my life, instead of the one that others expected from me." Interestingly, this is one of the main focuses of *Generative Change* and generative coaching—how to live your own life.

The second major regret was, "I wish I had not worked so hard." I've always found this one interesting because, for sure, I work a lot, but I never feel like I'm working hard. This is because I'm passionate about what I'm doing. I'm not doing it because I think I have to, or I should. I'm doing it because I want to. This is something we'll be working with a little bit more in this volume—finding a sense of *"passion"* and *"mission."*

The third most common regret was, "I wish I'd had the courage to express my feelings more." One of the key principles of generative change and generative coaching is to fully use our somatic wisdom. It is so easy in our world today to become disconnected from our feelings, from our body, and from our somatic intelligence and our emotional intelligence.

The fourth regret was, "I wish I had kept more contact with my friends." This relates to the notion of a *Generative Community*. There is an old saying that goes, "If you show me your friends, I'll show you your future." Obviously, in these times of social isolation, this becomes quite an important issue.

This fifth and final regret was, "I wish I had allowed myself to be happier." It is interesting that they didn't say, "I wish I had more opportunities to be happy." They said, "I didn't allow myself to be happy."

1. I wish I had the courage to *live a life true to myself*, not the one that others expected of me.

2. I wish that *I hadn't worked so hard*.

3. I wish I had the courage to *express my feelings*.

4. I wish I had *stayed in touch with my friends*.

5. I wish I had *let myself be happier*.

Creating a Future of No Regret

In Chapter 1, we took a deeper dive into the issue of *"aesthetic intelligence."* It seems clear that all these regrets are about something that is out of balance. Something is either "too much" or "not enough." So, a key part of our next prototype for **Step 2** is to bring attention to the significance of aesthetic intelligence.

An important consideration for ourselves and our clients, of course, is not to wait until we are dying, or in the process of dying, before we reflect and say, "Oh, what's out of balance?" We want to do that now. So, in this prototype, we look at some period into the future and, at the end of that period, whether it's one week, one month, or six months, we ask, "If I could look back with no regret, what would be different?" Applying the principles of aesthetic intelligence, what would need to change in order to bring more balance and more harmony? And by doing so we could say, "I have no regrets?" Or, from another perspective, we might say, "I don't know what's going to happen, I don't know how I am going to do it, but I know I would regret it if I don't go for it."

**If I could look back with no regret...
what would be different?**

Defining a Desired State of Greater Well-Being and No Regret

So, we are going to follow a basic set of steps but, as with all our generative change processes, this is not meant to be a rigid technique. It is intended to give you some guidelines that can be very helpful in a coaching session. The basic steps for the coachee are:

1. Create a physical timeline extending into your future

2. Enter the COACH State and move into the future on your timeline to a desired state of wellbeing. What would it be like to live in more balance and harmony, with no regret? What will you do more of? What will you do less of?

3. Identify the five words, an image or symbol, and a somatic expression that represent your intention.

4. From the future, turn to face the *you* in the present state. What belief does that you need in order to reach the desired state? What image and gesture goes with that belief?

5. Return to the present state, bringing the belief from your future self. Walk back up your timeline to the desired state as you experience that belief.

This process involves working with a physical timeline and requires enough space to take two or three steps into the future of that timeline. We are going to start in a COACH state and go into that future and create a future self who is going to be a kind of self-coach to our present self.

As usual, we are going to express this desired state in terms of five words, an image or symbol, and a somatic model. Once we have that future self, we are going to take something back to our present self. by asking, "What can I bring from this future self to my present self?" We are going to be anchoring it in the form of some kind of symbol. Especially interesting is, "What's the belief that I need to bring back to myself?" And "What is the symbol and somatic model that anchors that belief?"

Demonstration for Defining a Desired State of Greater Well-Being and No Regret

Robert: *Now, we're going to do our next demo. Hello James. Do you have some space where you would be able to move?*

James: *Yes.*

Robert: *One of the really important things when we start a virtual session like this is that you and I really come present in ourselves and have a good feeling of connection with each other. So, I'm curious if you would be willing to share an experience where you could really feel a state of flow, connection, and centered confidence? What is an experience that is a powerful resource for you?*

James: *I come from the world of business. I ran companies for more than twenty years. In terms of professional coaching, I'm still a rookie. So, when I am in a coaching session and I can help a person (especially someone who is from the business world) overcome their resistance to involving their body and begin to make gestures and somatic models that's really a great feeling.*

Robert: *So, let's take a moment to really connect to that great feeling. And, speaking of somatic models, what is your somatic model for that feeling?*

James: *It's just get on* [moves hands in a rotating motion in front of him], *keep on moving.*

Robert: [Mirrors the movement.] *Keep on moving. I like it.*

James: *Don't be desperate. Just look at what happens with the client and continue.*

Robert: *Beautiful. Just out of curiosity, on a scale of zero to ten, how strongly can you connect with that sense of moving on right now?*

James: *Nine.*

Robert: *Nine is great. I can feel that in the way you make this movement.*

So, James, the thing we want to work with in the session is to set an intention for a future of no regret. And, while we are not limited to them, there are some interesting guidelines by those five regrets of the dying people—living true to yourself, attaining a good work-life balance, expressing what you feel, staying in touch with friends and a good support system, and letting yourself be happy. This intention could be about your personal relationships, it could be about your work, it could be about your health, it could be about your emotions or any other area of your life that would be important to bring attention to at this time. Is there any particular part of your life that stands out, that would be most important to focus on?

James: *Yes, absolutely. About two years ago, for the first time, I founded my own company after working inside of big organizations for a long time. My company's mission is all about the "human side of change." That's why I was looking for the right way of coaching and came to generative coaching. We built it up pretty quickly over the last one and a half years and were on a positive track. We had some key successes and gathered a lot of good contacts. Then, this global lockdown happened. In times of crisis like this, the response of most companies is to cut costs by reducing their budgets—and things like coaching, consulting, and training are the first to go. I know it will be even more difficult over the months to come, and possibly far beyond that. It is not certain when companies will be ready to spend money on "the human side of change" again.*

Based on my experience as a leader inside big companies, I know how much value this approach can bring to businesses. And I am completely convinced, more than ever, that it is the right thing to do for organizations. I'm completely convinced and motivated, and that's my intention. I want to bring this to companies, because they need it, and I know it works. But I also know that time is limited and I can't wait one and a year or however long the crisis lasts, to continue. This type of work needs to be spread into the market. They need to be convinced and open up their minds to be ready to follow this path. That's what I would like to achieve.

Robert: *So, you would like to continue building your business based on "the human side of change" in the face of these big challenges where companies have reduced budgets and are putting things off. This is where this frame of "no regret" becomes really important. We can't control what is happening in the world, but we can choose what we do and what we put our energy into.*

I'd like to invite you to think about a time frame—the end of the year, for example—and imagine you were able to say, "Regardless of what's happened or how far I've gotten, I have a sense of balance and wellbeing. I know that I've done what I'm here to do and I have no regret." Sound interesting?

James: *Yes, absolutely.*

Robert: *Great. Let's just take a moment and first just do a little bit of COACH State Tai Chi together.* [Makes the series of gestures as he speaks. James mirrors the movements.] *Centering . . . opening . . . alert and aware . . . especially connecting, so that you're really in that place of being ready. And maybe you can add that gesture you were sharing of that sense of "okay, we're on the way!"* [Moves hands in a rotating motion in front of him.]

James: [Mirrors the movement and smiles broadly.]

Robert: *And from there, take these two or three steps in the future that would represent something like until the end of the year. It doesn't have to be a precise date, but someplace where you feel, "I've been able to do all I can to create what I wanted to create, no regret. I feel balanced and in harmony with the life I want to live." When you're ready, move into that future.*

James: [Takes several steps, continuing to move his hands in a rotating motion in front of him.]

Robert: *Really take that opportunity to really arrive there. To really feel like, "This is what I want. This is where I want to go. No matter what's happened, I can truly say, 'I have no regret'." If you could really get that sense, how would you express that in five words or less?*

James: *I will go on, following this way.*

Robert: *Let's explore a little bit more about what "this way" means. What will you be doing more of or less of?*

James: *I will be doing more of one-to-one conversations with potential clients.*

Robert: *Great. Is there anything that you would be doing less of?*

James: *I will be less concerned that it may take too long.*

Robert: *So, more one-to-one conversation with clients, and less concern that there's not going to be enough time. Is that enough for you to be able to look back with no regret? So, no matter what has happened, you can say, "I've done my best." What would really bring that sense of wellbeing with no regret?*

James: *Well, it's finding a way to open the door for clients to move into this new approach. And having the courage to try.*

Robert: *Yes, having the courage to try. Having the one-on-one conversations that open the door to a new approach and having the courage to keep trying to open that door. I'm curious, as you let that resonate through you, is there some kind of image or picture that comes to you of these courageous conversations?*

James: *There's an image coming up of a wave approaching the shore, and getting bigger and bigger before it breaks.*

Robert: *Yes, I see that and* [takes a deep breath] *I feel it. What's your gesture for this?*

James: *It's the power that goes with the wave.* [Moves his hands and arms in a wave-like gesture out in front of him.]

Robert: [Mirrors the movement.] *This is very interesting because you had your resource gesture for moving ahead.* [Moves hands in a rotating motion.] *And this adds another whole dimension to that, which seems to be about being carried by something bigger than you.* [Moves his hands and arms in a wave-like gesture out in front of him.]

James: [Makes the wave-like gesture.] *Yes. It is as if this is something that is inevitable. Nothing can stop it.*

Robert: *Great! Let's put all these parts together. As you visualize that wave and make the gesture, how would you state your intention?*

James: [Moves his hands and arms in a wave-like gesture out in front of him.] *I want to have more one-to-one conversations with potential clients and courage.*

Robert: *So, more one-on-one conversations to potential clients and courage.* [Mirrors James' movement.] *Fantastic. Now, I'd like to invite you to turn back toward the James in the "present." From here in your future, you're looking back to this present James who wants to reach this desired state that you are experiencing. If you were the coach to that present James, what is the belief that you would really want to make sure that he has, in order to get where you are in his future? What's your message to him? What is the belief that he needs to have in order to achieve this desired state?*

James: *Trust in you. Trust in what you think, in what you do, what you see, what you know. You have your own experience, and you know how it feels there in the business, and what the means and opportunities are.*

Robert: *So, "Trust in yourself. Trust in what you see, what you think, and what you know. You have the experience. It's the right way to go." What would be your image or your somatic model for that trust?*

James: [Opens his hands and makes a repeated gesture as if encouraging someone to move forward.] *Keep pushing. Keep pushing, don't compare. Go on, keep on pushing.*

Robert: [Mirrors the gesture.] *"Keep pushing, don't compare. Go on."*

So, now, we're going to take that back to the beginning of your timeline. [Accompanies James as they take several steps back.] *And look up your timeline to the future you who has achieved this desired state of having more conversations with potential clients and less concern that it may take too long. Even in an uncertain future, what is certain is that there's "you" in that future. There is a "you" who is* *finding a way to open the door for the clients to move into this new approach based on the human side of change and who has the courage to try. And this future you is telling you here in the present, "Trust in you. You have the experience. Trust in what you think, in what you do, what you see, and what you know."* [Opens his hands and makes a repeated gesture as if encouraging someone to move forward.] *"Keep pushing. Keep pushing, don't compare. Go on, keep on pushing."* As you receive that message, where would you most need to have that in your body?*

James: [Places his hands over his heart.]

Robert: *Really sense that belief there that you can trust in you and your experience, and keep on pushing ahead, without comparing.*

James: [Breathes deeply and nods his head.]

Robert: *Now what we want to do is to step again to your future bringing that trust and courage to keep pushing ahead.* [Opens his hands and makes a repeated gesture as if encouraging someone to move forward.]

James: [Mirrors the gesture as he walks several steps, then stops, breathes deeply, and smiles broadly.]

Robert: *Now, let's come back to the present.* [Accompanies James as they take several steps back.] *The next step in the **generative coaching process** would be to go into a **generative state** and start working out the specific action steps. However, I think this is a good place to stop for now, and let the work we just did settle in. And I just want you to know that I send you my full support.*

James: *Thank you very much.* [Smiles broadly.]

Robert: *Before we wrap up, is there anything that you would like to share about what was important for you with respect to this session?*

James: *Yes, definitely. Thinking in terms of what there would be more of and less of really helped me to get clearer about what I wanted to do and what it would be like. And then, exploring what I would need in order make that happen—the courage and the trust, was really important. It became very clear what I would need in the present moment to get going and follow through. So, it was just one step following the other. That works very well with me. It was very helpful. Thank you.*

Defining a Desired State of Greater Well Being and No Regret

4) DISCOVER THE WORDS, IMAGE AND SOMATIC MODEL FOR YOUR FUTURE.

5) GIVE YOURSELF A MESSAGE FROM THE FUTURE.

6) INTEGRATE.

Reflection on the Process

This process gives another prototype for **Step 2** of the generative coaching method—*Setting a Goal/Intention*. This prototype can be especially useful for setting intentions in contexts of significant uncertainty and change. At a deeper structure level, James' situation was a classic example that has probably been experienced by many of us. You're starting something and building something new and then, suddenly, the whole world as we know it is different. And we don't know how long that's going to last. What do we ground in when everything else is changing? How do we keep our sense of direction even though everything seems uncertain?

We usually experience these situations as a *"crisis."* However, I always like to keep in mind the Chinese character for crisis, which is a combination of two other characters. One character is *"danger"* and the other is *"opportunity."* Usually, the dangers and the constraints are obvious. As James was pointing out in his situation, companies are cutting back their budgets and there's a lot of panic and contraction. Interestingly, though, there are probably an equal amount of opportunities. James was realizing this when he said, "What I want to do is important. It's as valuable now as ever."

The Chinese character for crisis is the combination of the characters for "danger" and "opportunity".

Part of setting an intention is creating one that is clear and powerful enough that we are willing and able to "stay the course"—i.e., keep focused on that direction and remain committed to that path. In this particular prototype, we work with the two key points of the present and the future. We create a timeline that connects the future and the present. And rather than try to set the intention in the present thinking about the future, we're projecting ourselves into the future and experiencing what the desired state will be like.

The question that we are exploring as we do this, which relates very much to the notion of aesthetic intelligence, is "What will there be more of or less of?" As we could see in the work with James, the answer frequently starts with something fairly concrete, i.e., "more conversations with potential clients." As you explore further, you will typically begin to uncover the inner processes that produce those concrete actions, such as "more courage, and less concern about time."

We could also see the importance of aesthetic intelligence in James' movement toward his desired state in the form of what we would call "generative complementarities." On one side, he was being carried by a wave of something bigger than himself that seemed inevitable. On the other side, he was encouraging and pushing himself. So, one part of it involved opening and connecting to the energy of a bigger field. The other part came from personal commitment and determination.

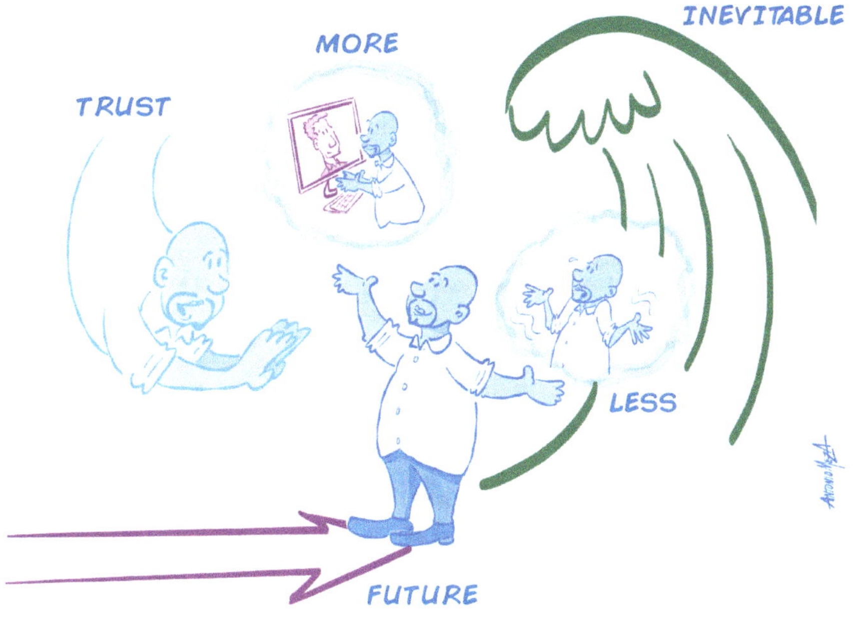

One thing that we are doing in this process that is a little different than the typical prototype for *Setting Intention* is to bring a belief from the future desired state back to the present. As James reflected at the end of his session, it's often really important to make that connection: "What is that belief that I need in order to be able to get from the present to my desired state in the future?" James, for example, talked about trust in himself, in his experience and that what he was doing was the "right way to go."

It is important to locate the belief somewhere in the body, so that it's not just words or an abstract idea. A belief is more than a cognitive formulation; it is something that resonates through our somatic intelligence. In fact, one of the things we will be looking at more in the coming chapters is the linking and alignment between the head, the heart, and the belly.

The final step of this process is to go from the present back up the timeline with that resource to the future desired state, again linking the present to the future. Now, what's happening there is, we don't know all of the specific actions and details necessary to achieve that desired state—that we get to in **Step 4**—but it makes clear that "this is the direction, this is the path."

It is important for the coach to mirror back the client's words and gestures.

As with any step in the *generative coaching process*, it is important for the coach to mirror back the client's words and gestures. This is key for making connection and strengthening the coach-client field, especially when working virtually. And it is important to keep in mind that, as the coach, the care for that field always starts with you. As our colleague and friend Richard Moss likes to point out, *"The distance between you and anybody else, is the same as the distance between you and yourself."* So, if I'm not connected to me, it's impossible for me to be truly connected to you. If I am disconnected from myself, I can't connect to anybody else. That is why centering in our COACH State is so important.

Of course, there is a natural "learning curve" to whatever we are doing. Whether it is working virtually or having people make somatic models, almost anything that you do that is new is going to feel awkward and unfamiliar at first. But, as we always like to remind our clients, "Anything worth doing, is worth doing imperfectly at first." None of us are going to ride a bicycle perfectly the first time.

As you are practicing these steps of generative coaching, we really hope that you can relax and begin to welcome the awkwardness. It is worth it. We truly believe, as James was saying in his session, that even if people don't realize it yet, generative change is exactly what the world needs most right now. If you can know that in your being, not just as an idea or a thought, but when you can know that in your head, heart and gut, then you become a real change agent in the world.

Keep in mind that, as the coach, the care for the field starts with you.

INDECISION

Friend, please,
Do not try to decide now.
Do not shut any possibility out of your heart.

Honor this place of not-knowing.
Bow before this bubbling mess of creativity.

Slow down. Breathe.
Sink into wonderment.
Befriend the very place where you stand.

Any decision will make itself, in time.
Any choice will happen when your deffences are down.
Answers will appear only when they are ready.
When the questions have been fully honored, and loved.

Do not label this place 'indecision'.
It is more alive than that.
It is a place where possibilities grow.
It is a place where uncertainty is sacred.

There is courage in staying close.
There is strength in not knowing.

Friend, please know,
There is simply no choice now.

Except to breathe, and breathe again,
And trust this Intelligence beyond mind.

—Jeff Foster

Chapter 4

Step 3—Developing a Generative State

In this chapter, we are going to work with deepening and enriching Step 3 of the Generative Coaching process—*Developing a Generative State*. The poem for this chapter is by a British author and spiritual teacher named Jeff Foster, titled *Indecision*. This poem is essentially about the importance and power of a generative state. Even though many of us would think of uncertainty as being something that is a problem or a challenge, we like to say that the state of *not knowing* is actually a very important part of generative change. In generative change, we are always letting something come to us, come through us, and letting something emerge.

In the poem, we hear about how, through the experience of "not knowing," our cognitive mind opens up to a place of intelligence beyond itself, beyond the mind. In times of great personal, individual and global uncertainty, this is very wise advice for us. It means making decisions from more than just our rational cognitive intelligence. One of our big lessons for this chapter is going to be about the notion of alignment, beginning with the alignment of head, heart, and our gut or belly. Oftentimes, we regret something when we make the decision from only one of these places.

Wisdom does not come from rationality alone. It comes from accessing all of our intelligences. As the poem is implying, if we rush to a choice or rush to a decision without holding that place of "sacred uncertainty," then that we might make choices or take actions that we will regret. Developing the courage and the strength to do this is where beliefs come into the process. In the demonstration with James in the previous chapter, the beliefs that he could "trust himself," "trust his experience" and that what he was doing was "the right way to go," were key for him to effectively address and deal with the uncertainties related to his intention.

Similarly, in the demonstration with Kate in Chapter 2, the beliefs that she could "succeed even if she felt a bit overwhelmed" and that "everything would be fine" when facing a challenging situation, were essential for her to face the uncertainties of "putting herself out onto the market."

As we have established in the previous volumes of *Generative Coaching*, our fundamental prototype for developing a generative state is establishing the three positive connections—(1) to our center, (2) to our intention, and (3) to our field of resources.

In this chapter, we will show we can use certain key beliefs to strengthen each of these connections.

The Three Positive Connections of a Generative State

Introduction to Beliefs

Beliefs have a profound impact on our inner state. Beliefs can be either generative or degenerative. There are beliefs that will put our filters into a generative state and there are going to be beliefs that will shut down our filters.

A belief is a classic example of what can be called a "neuro-linguistic program." We often express beliefs in verbal language but they are more than words and more than thoughts. They are words or thoughts that influence the state of our nervous system, and thus our filters—which determine our reality. Words and verbal language are formed in our brain and have a strong influence on our brain and how we think. But the most powerful thoughts and beliefs are going to influence other parts of our nervous system.

In the demonstrations with both Kate and James, they indicated that the place where they most strongly experienced their key beliefs was in the belly. So, it's not just a thought that's in the head. When our words are resonant with our bodies, then other filters are activated and can potentially come into a generative state.

The Three Belief Centers

In the generative change model, we identify three fundamental neurological centers for processing our experience of the world, and which can produce the resonance needed for belief. We view (1) the head as being the center for reason and for planning; (2) the heart tends to be more about passion, connection and compassion; and (3) the belly tends to be more about our inner world, including intuition and often evaluation.

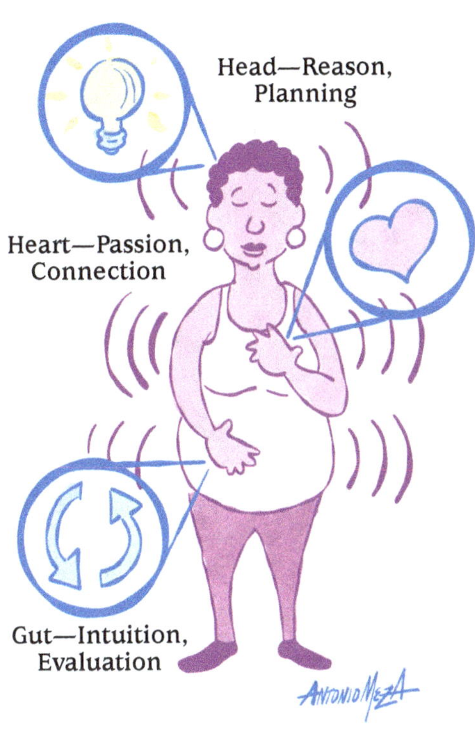

The Three Basic Belief Centers

There are neurological reasons for all of this. For instance, it makes sense that reason and planning would be in the head because, if you think about it, all of the so-called distance receptors are up in the head—the eyes, the ears, the nose and the mouth. Everything that connects us to the outer world tends to be up in the head. Neuroscientists are also continually learning more and more about all of the sophisticated networks of nerves around the heart and the networks of nerves around the belly—what they call the "enteric nervous system." While the head links us to the outer world, the belly is more attuned to our inner world. The heart is in between the head and the gut. Thus, the heart tends to reflect the connection between our inner world and the outer world.

In this chapter, we're going to be exploring how a belief is not just the words, and it's not just the thought. It's the level of resonance that something has through these different parts of our nervous system. When a belief can bring these different parts of our filters into a generative state—when my intellect is generative, my sense of passion and connection is generative, my sense of intuition and evaluation is generative—then I'm going to be able to really create something new and respond effectively to whatever is occurring.

The Power of Beliefs in Generative Change

One of the main purposes of belief is to create a new reality. Before we can create a flying machine, for instance, we have to believe it is possible to make a machine that can fly. Similarly, in order to heal something, develop a particular quality of relationship, make a certain amount of money, etc., I have to begin by believing that I can do it. If don't believe that I can do something or that it's possible, I won't even try it.

Thus, beliefs can play a very powerful role in how we live our lives and create our realities. A classic example of the impact of belief is the so-called "placebo effect." Somebody can take a pill that has no active biological agent in it, a sugar pill for example, and they can have dramatic responses in their body. It's not just that the person thinks that they are better, they actually can have remarkable physiological results from a pill that has no active ingredient in it.

Beliefs tend to create an expectation—but it is not just a cognitive expectation. It's something that can resonate through the whole nervous system. Placebos, for example, can be used as a substitute for almost any drug and they all have some kind of an effect. Actually, one of the interesting things about placebos is that they can also produce side effects. A particularly dramatic example of this comes from a study where they gave women placebo chemotherapy for breast cancer. They injected them with a solution that had no medication in it, but were told it was a powerful drug. Astonishingly, one-third of the women that got the placebo chemotherapy lost all of their hair! There was no drug in the solution, and yet a significant percentage of the patients lost all of their hair because they believed and expected that it would happen.

This shows how deeply resonant beliefs can go into the body, and also how they can produce degenerative as well as generative effects. It illustrates, for instance, just how strongly a limiting belief or some kind of negative expectation can influence us.

The Placebo Effect

Basic Beliefs Relating to Change

We are going to go over the basic beliefs relating to change that we typically work with in generative coaching. Then we will describe and demonstrate how we bring these positive, empowering, beliefs into Step 3 of the generative coaching process.

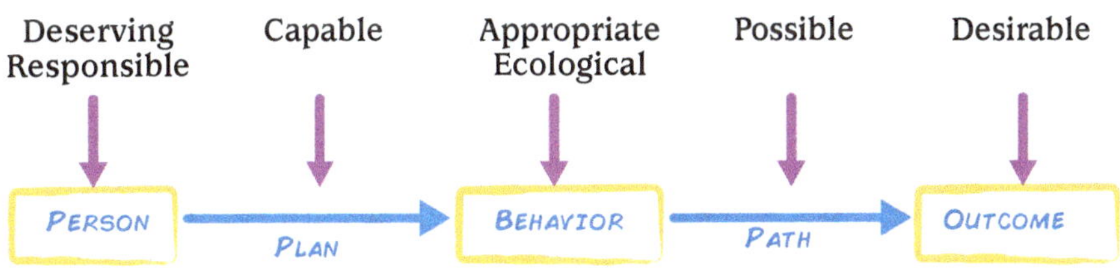

Basic Beliefs Relating to Change

Desirability of the Intention/Outcome

There are several areas where beliefs can have a strong influence on the process of change. One of these areas would be about the outcome, or intention, that we are trying to achieve. The most important belief there is that the intention, or the outcome, is important and it's worth it—that I really want it. It is something that's important and it's worth all of the effort, the risks, and everything else that's going to have to go into achieving it. Because if it's not important and I don't really want it, I'm going to give up as soon as I start meeting obstacles.

Deserving

In the beginning of the demonstration with James in the previous chapter, for example, there was a point where he stated, "Based on my experience as a leader inside big companies, I know how much value this approach can bring to businesses. And I am completely convinced, more than ever, that it is the right thing to do for organizations." This is a good example of a strong belief in the desirability of his intention to continue bringing "the human side of change" to companies and organizations.

Let's say a client says something like, "My intention is to make X amount of money." One question is going to be, "How important is it for you to have that amount of money?" If the client goes, "Oh, well it would be nice. Then I would be rich." You can bet you're in for a lot of trouble. If, on the other hand, the person says, "I need that amount of money not only for my own survival but to provide for my family so we can get by and thrive," that's going to be a much more significant and motivating statement of intention.

This is where the issue of values becomes connected with beliefs. Language like "making money" and "being rich" is more about the level of behavior and environment, and primarily in service of the "ego." It is relatively abstract and doesn't typically produce a great deal of resonance in the body. "Survival" and "providing for my family," are more about the levels of identity and mission or purpose, which is more likely to resonate more deeply to other belief centers than the head.

Possibility to Achieve the Intention/Outcome

Let's say that the client does state, "Well, it's vitally important that I am able to make at least that amount of money." The next question is going to become, "Is it possible to make that amount of money? Is it even possible to produce that amount of money, in the amount of time available?" If I say, "I want to make ten million dollars by tomorrow morning," is that even possible regardless of how much you want it?

As we pointed out earlier, the belief in possibility is very important for generative change. Before we can send somebody to the Moon, we have to believe it's possible to get to the moon. Even if we don't know how to do it right now, we still believe that it's possible. That is what drives the efforts to create the way to do it.

The demonstration with James in the previous chapter also provides a good illustration of the importance of this belief. When considering the challenges and uncertainty relating to his intention for his new company, the image came up for James of a wave approaching the shore, and getting bigger and bigger before it broke. As he pointed out, this represented to him the belief that his intention/outcome was "something that is inevitable" and that "nothing can stop it."

Capable

Appropriateness of the Behavior/Path

Let's say the client we have been using as an example congruently says, "I want to make X amount of money. It is really important and worth the effort. And I believe it's possible to do that." The next question is about how and in what way that is going to be achieved. This is where the example of the placebo effect becomes relevant. If somebody really believes that this "medicine" is going to make a difference for them, it most likely will. So this has to do with the approach that is being taken to achieve the intention or outcome, rather than whether the intention is desirable or possible.

As an illustration, a fascinating study was done some years ago in which some researchers were interviewing long-term cancer survivors. They interviewed something like two hundred people who had been given a terminal diagnosis of cancer, yet they survived. They were given only a certain number of months to live, but they all had some sort of remarkable recovery and ten to fifteen years later, they were still alive and, in most cases, thriving.

The question was, what did they do? The researchers figured, "If we can find out what they all did, then we can improve treatments for other cancer patients." To their consternation, however, what they found was that none of them had done the same thing. They all did different things. Some did traditional medical treatments; others changed their diets or took an alternative approach. Some took supplements. Some went to healers or said prayers, or did other special kinds of either religious or psychological practices. In fact, the only thing that was common to all of the 200 patients, was that they believed, *"What I am doing will work for me."* They believed in what they were doing.

Appropriate/Ecological

This is a profound discovery that relates directly to generative change and generative coaching. We have worked with people for more than forty-five years and have developed many techniques of our own. What we know is, if people believe in the technique and they believe in us, it will probably work easily and well. If they don't believe in it, it is going to be a struggle for both of us.

This area of belief came up in the demonstration with James when his future self sent the message, "It's the right way to go," to his present self. The implication was that the behavior/path he was taking was appropriate; that he was headed in the right direction.

Capability to Do What is Needed

This takes us to the next area of belief about capability. "Am I capable to do what I need to do in order to get that outcome?" In our example about somebody with the intention to make a certain amount of money, they might say, "Yeah, it is desirable, it is possible, and here is the way to do it but I don't think that I am capable to do that." So, it is not a belief about the intention, and it is not a belief about the action or path, it's a belief about themselves and their capability.

For example, one of the big paradoxes of the placebo effect is that if you tell the patient, "Hey, guess what? You got well but it's a fake drug. It's not the drug, it's you that's doing it." What happens is, the placebo stops working and the symptoms return. That is the paradox. If you tell the person taking the placebo that it is a placebo, it almost invariably stops working. Why? Because the person doesn't believe in their own capability. They believe in medicine, in something outside of themselves.

Now, for all coaching and especially generative coaching, this is crucial. If your client does not believe in their own capability and they only believe in you and your technique, then you are not truly coaching. An effective coach empowers their clients to reach their intentions and outcomes. We know we have done a good job when our client says, "Thank you. I can take it from here."

Possible

This area of belief has to do with key questions such as, "Am I capable to do what needs to be done? Do I have the intelligence, the resources, the competence to be able to do what needs to be done to reach my intention?" In the demonstration with James, this belief showed up in the message from his future self to "Trust in what you think, in what you do, what you see, what you know. You have your own experience, and you know how it feels there in the business, and what the means and opportunities are." The message was essentially, "You are capable."

Self-Worth and Responsibility

Finally, there is a key area of belief that relates to yourself, but not about your capabilities. It's more about your identity and your sense of self-worth. It involves questions such as, "Do I deserve it?" and "Am I the one who is responsible to do it?" This area of belief is a type of complement to the first belief area regarding "Is the intention worth it?" The issue here is, "Am I worthy and worth it?" This is where people confront obstacles such as, "Why should you be the one to achieve this intention? What makes you so special? Who do you think you are?"

Desirable

In the conclusion of the demonstration with James, for instance, the issue of self-worth and responsibility was addressed by his statement to himself to, "Keep pushing, don't compare. Go on," as well as his message to, "Trust in you." The implication of these statements was that he was worthy and responsible to achieve his intention with respect to his business.

If we go back to our example about earning money, this area of belief would involve questions such as, "Do I deserve to make that amount of money? Why should I make that much money? Am I good enough? Am I worthy of it?" It also tends to bring up the issue of responsibility. "Is it my responsibility to do it?" Someone might have the objection, "Well, it is not me that should do it. It is "the government," "top management," "other family members," etc., that should be providing financial security."

Lack of self-worth can be one of the biggest obstacles that prevents people from achieving their desired outcomes. On the other hand, a strong feeling of worthiness and responsibility empowers people to be determined, persistent and generative.

Basic Belief Statements

We can summarize these key beliefs with the following statements:

1. *My intention is important and worth the effort and risk.* **I want it. It is worth it**.

2. **It is possible** *to achieve my intention.* **It can be done.**

3. *The actions/direction I am taking are/is appropriate to achieve my intention.* **What I am doing will work.**

4. *I have the capabilities to achieve my intention.* **I can do it.**

5. *I deserve and take responsibility to achieve my intention.* **I am worth it. I will do it.**

These statements constitute the "linguistic" aspect of these beliefs. The degree to which we actually believe them is determined by the degree of resonance they produce in the head, heart and gut. Thus, when we are coaching we are not necessarily using these exact statements, as it's not about these specific words. It's about finding resonant words.

Relationship of the Basic Beliefs for Change to the Three Positive Connections

Reflecting on these five areas of belief, it is evident that the first two beliefs support a positive connection to the intention itself: *"My intention is important and worth it,"* and *"It is possible to achieve it."*

The third belief area, *"The actions/direction I am taking are/is appropriate to achieve my intention,"* is about the connection between myself and my intention. This belief area becomes particularly important during Step 4 of the Generative Coaching process, when we are moving into action.

The fourth and fifth areas of belief—that *"I am capable to achieve my intention"* and that *"I am worthy and responsible"*—have to do with strengthening a positive connection with myself.

This brings us to the final positive connection—to my field of resources. This is where we will often add a sixth area of belief characterized by the statement, *"I have permission and support to achieve my intention."* This serves to remind us and connect us to the bigger field of resources that we will need to ultimately achieve our intention.

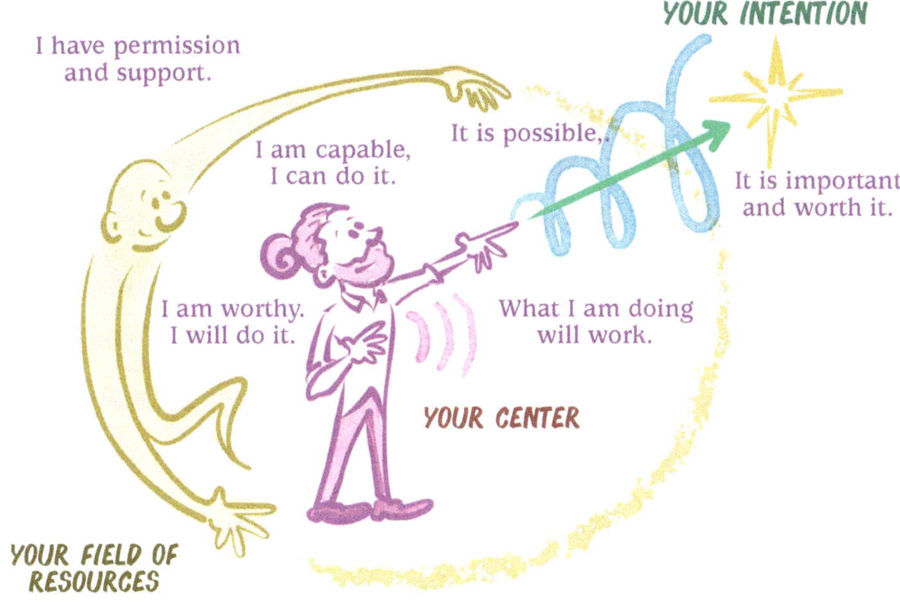

Relationship of the Basic Beliefs for Change to the
Three Positive Connections

Coaching Belief

In the Generative Coaching process, once we have completed the first two steps of opening a **COACH** field between the coach and client, then helping the client to define his or her intention, the third step is to develop a generative state. This involves establishing the three connections to (1) *intention*, (2) *self* and (3) the *field of resources*.

To strengthen the three connections, we bring in these various areas of belief. "Do I believe in my intention? Do I really want that intention? Do I believe it's possible? Do I believe that the direction I am taking is appropriate? Do I believe that I am capable to do what is necessary to achieve the intention? Do I believe that I deserve it and am responsible to accomplish it? Do I have the support from my field of resources?"

Basic Prototype for Coaching Beliefs

The basic prototype that we use to coach beliefs such as these is:

1. After getting into COACH State and establishing your intention, identify several reference experiences for a strong level of belief and calibrate how you know it in the head, heart and belly.

2. Say each belief statement out loud and check the degree of resonance (on a scale of zero to ten) in the head, heart and gut. Notice which ones are rated below seven and in which part of the body greater resonance is needed.

3. For any statement that is rated below seven, identify a role model or mentor from your field of resources who can support you to strengthen or increase the level of resonance or confidence. Experience the presence of the role model or mentor and the message or resource they bring that supports the needed area of belief.

e = mc²
"I AM CAPABLE"
10 9 8 7 6 5 4 3 2 1
"I AM LESS CAPABLE"
10 9 8 7 6 5 4 3 2 1
"I AM A BIT
MORE CAPABLE"
10 9 8 7 6 5 4 3 2 1

Demonstration of Strengthening the Generative State with Beliefs

The following is a transcript of a demonstration that Robert did as part of a virtual training course.

Martha: *Hi Robert. I am really glad to see you.*

Robert: *Martha, thank you for being our demo for this. I think we can do something that is going to be really helpful and useful for you. Of course, before we go into anything with belief, we will do our COACH State and find out what is the intention that you would like to create.*

Opening the COACH Field

A good way to start is to do a little COACH State Tai Chi together. Let us both center. [Robert and Martha make centering gesture together.] And then let us open especially opening our heart center and really experiencing that space that connects us even if we are physically far away. [Robert and Martha make opening gesture together.] Let us be alert and aware. [Robert and Martha make gesture for awareness together.] Then let us connect to ourselves; to the head, to the heart, to the belly and to the whole body. [Robert and Martha make connecting gesture together.] And then hold that space between us so we can both feel present and also a sense of connection to each other. [Robert and Martha make holding gesture together.] When we can sense that we are in our COACH state, at least seven out of a scale of zero to ten we can say, "I am ready."

Martha: *I am ready, and it is like seven, exactly seven.*

Robert: *Okay, and I see you. I am wondering, if we could get a little bit more than seven, what would it be?*

Martha: *I really like these active centering exercises. I found them really useful. I started standing on one leg. It is amazing. I stand on my leg and check. [Martha balances herself on one leg.] Now, it is eight.*

Establishing the Intention

Robert: *Great. Let us go now to the intention. Think about taking a step or two to your future and asking yourself, "What is it that I most want to create?" As you look to your future, what is something that is going to be really important for you and useful for you to create more?*

Martha: *I really need to learn how to take care of myself because now, the situation is that I need to support a lot of people, and sometimes, I lose track of caring about myself, about my health, about my mood, and state. I really want to remember to do that.*

Robert: *Let us put that into five words. What would be your five words for that? What would be your basic way to say that intention?*

Martha: *I want to take care of myself, to trust myself, and to love myself.* [Brings her hand to her belly.]

Robert: *So, "to take care of myself, to trust myself, to love myself." I can see, by the way already, that your hand is touching down here.* [Gestures to her belly.] *"To take care of myself, to trust myself, to love myself." As you really breathe that intention through you, what image comes to you of that intention?*

Martha: *I am running. I see myself running through the forest.*

Robert: *Awesome. I am a runner, and run everyday, so I am like, "Oh, yeah!" What would be your gesture for this intention . . . of "take care of myself, trust myself, love myself"?*

Martha: *It is like sitting down with my hands on my heart and my belly.* [Places her hands over her heart and belly.]

Robert: *Yeah. I like that.* [Mirrors the gesture.]

This gesture is a nice complement to the image of running in the forest. It feels like a nice balance.

Martha: *Yes, it feels good.* [Smiles broadly.]

Robert: *So, let us put all these three together. Make the gesture, see the image, and say that intention.*

Martha: [Places her hands over her heart and belly.] *I want to take care of myself, to trust myself, and to love myself.*

Robert: *Beautiful. Martha, as you say that, how strongly do you feel your connection to that intention right now, on a scale of zero to ten?*

Martha: *I want to take care of myself, trust myself, and love myself . . . and now I want to pat myself.* [Smiles and begins to pat her heart, belly, face and arms.]

Robert: *Great. How strongly can you feel your connection to that now?*

Martha: *Seven.*

Robert: *Good. And how strongly can you feel a connection to yourself and your center?*

Martha: *Eight.*

Finding Resources

Robert: *Wonderful. Now, for Step 3, we also start with finding some resources. If you open to your field of resources, who or what resources are most important for you to be able to truly take care of yourself, trust yourself, and love yourself?*

Martha: *I have some images of several people and then, I got this image of a cat.*

Robert: *Of a cat?*

Martha: *Of a cat, yes. Because it can take care of herself. It can lick herself and be loving to herself.* [Smiles and gestures as if licking her paws like a cat.]

Robert: *Right. Great. Let us say welcome to this cat. If you really were to sense your connection to this cat and this cat quality, where would you most sense that in your body?*

Martha: *Yes. Somewhere like here.* [Folds her arms in front of her as if holding something precious.]

Robert: *Yeah, great.* [Mirrors the gesture.] *How strongly can you feel that connection right now to this cat and this cat quality?*

Martha: *It is like nine.*

Robert: *Fabulous. What kind of cat is it by the way?*

Martha: *It is a big, Siberian, red cat.*

Robert: [Folds his arms in front of him as if holding something precious.] *"Welcome" to this big, Siberian, red cat.*

Martha: [Continues making the gesture and smiles broadly.]

Finding Reference Experiences for Belief

Robert: *Now, Martha, in a moment we are going to add in some beliefs. But before we do, I want to invite you to find some reference experiences for belief. It is important to keep in mind that a true belief is quite different from a thought, a hope or a wish. Wanting to believe something or thinking "I should believe it" is not the same as actually believing it. This is why it is important to get some clear reference experiences for when you actually congruently believed something.*

So, I would like to just invite you to briefly reflect on your life and your experiences and find an example or maybe several examples of when you really believed that something was important and was worth it. You really wanted it and you knew it was possible and appropriate for you. And you were right. It was possible. And you also knew you were capable to get it and that you deserved it; that you would do it. And you were right. You were able to do it and you did it. See what you saw, hear what you heard and feel what you felt in that experience. Put yourself into that energy of belief. How do you experience that sense of certainty, congruence and confidence? Check your head, your heart, and your belly. Really tune in to the experience of belief in your body. What is your somatic model for this deep quality of belief?

Martha: [Lengthens her spine, opens her chest and extends her hands in front of her with both thumbs up.] *I have my shoulders open and there is this decisiveness and clear movements.*

Going Through the Six Belief Statements

Robert: [Mirrors the gesture.] *Fantastic. Good to know. I can really see and sense a deep quality of congruence when you do that. So, let's start with your intention. I am going to invite you to say, "It is important and worth it to me to take care of myself, trust myself and love myself." See the image of yourself running in the forest and make your gesture for belief followed by the gesture for your intention.* [Robert demonstrates by lengthening his spine, opening his chest and extending his hands with both thumbs up, and then placing his hands over his heart and belly.]

Martha: *Okay. For me, it is important to learn how to take care of myself, to trust myself, to love myself.* [Lengthens her spine, opens her chest and extends her hands in front of her with both thumbs up, then places her hands over her heart and belly.]

Robert: *As you check your head, your heart and your belly, how strongly do you feel the resonance?*

Martha: *It is very strong. I would say eight or nine.*

Robert: *Yes. I can see and sense that. Now let us do the second belief, which is, "It is possible for me to learn to take care of myself, trust myself and love myself."*

Martha: [Shoulders tense up and jaw tightens.] *As soon as you say, "It is possible," I can feel something inside of me saying, "No. I've been there. I've tried it all. It is never going to happen."*

Robert: *First of all, let us say welcome to that. I am sure it makes sense. That is interesting. I am sure there's something there that is needing to be heard, held or healed. Welcome. And where do you feel that in your body?*

Martha: *Somewhere here in my belly.* [Closes her fists and gestures to her abdomen.]

Robert: *Yeah, in your belly.* [Mirrors her gesture.] *Again, we want to say, "I am sure this makes sense; that there's something important here." At the same time, what we want to do is to stay connected to your center. Even with this voice inside of you saying, "It is never going to happen," you can stay connected to an even deeper presence, like that big Siberian red cat.* [Folds his arms in front of him as if holding something precious.]

Martha: [Mirrors the gesture.] *Yes. I can feel myself centered. And I just felt that this gesture* [Closes her fists and gestures to her abdomen.] *is somehow connected with my center in my belly, and they are on the same ground.*

Robert: *So if we make this gesture and stay centered . . .* [Mirrors the gesture in a slow relaxed way.] *I am curious, what do you become aware of?*

Martha: [Closes her fists and makes a repeated gesture to her abdomen in a slow rhythmic movement.] *It was like, "No." And then it transforms into some kind of a movement.*

Robert: *That is interesting. And I am curious when you make this movement* [mirrors the movement], *what do you experience?*

Martha: [Repeats the gesture slowly and attentively.] *It is a movement of certainty. I like this movement. I know that I am certain of something.*

Robert: *That is very interesting. So this movement itself is an important team member. Welcome! I am also curious Martha, what happens if you bring your red Siberian cat here?*

Martha: [Folds her arms in front of her as if holding something precious and begins to make a petting motion.] *I am kind of petting it.*

Robert: *What message does this cat have for you about this belief that it is possible for you to learn to take care of yourself, trust yourself and love yourself? It may not be in words.*

Martha: *It is something like, "It is natural and normal to take care of yourself and to love and trust yourself. Keep me close. I will show you how."*

Robert: *That sounds like a great resource. So now, what happens if you say, "It is possible for me to learn to take care of myself, to trust myself and to love myself?" And make your gesture.* [Opens his chest and extends his hands in front of him with both thumbs up, then places his hands over his heart and belly.]

Martha: [Mirrors the gesture.] *It is important and possible to learn how to take care of myself and love myself and trust myself.* [Smiles broadly.] *Now I am certain of it!*

Robert: *That is nice. Breathe that through. It is important and it is possible. Now next, this belief is that it is appropriate to take care of yourself, love yourself and trust yourself. You will be going into more detail about the specifics of the actions in Step 4 at a later time, so for now just focus on the intention to move in the direction of taking care of yourself, trusting yourself and loving yourself. Connect to your center, to that intention and, of course, to the cat. Say the belief out loud, "It is appropriate to take care of myself, trust myself and love myself." Picture yourself running in the forest and make your gesture for belief.*

Martha: *It is appropriate to take care of myself, trust myself and love myself.* [Lengthens her spine, opens her chest and extends her hands in front of her with both thumbs up, then places her hands over her heart and belly.]

Robert: *Check how strongly that resonates in your head, heart and belly.*

Martha: *This is quite strong. I would say it is easily eight.*

Robert: *Great. Now the next belief is "I am capable to do what I need to." It is different than "It is possible." It is, "I am capable to learn to take care of myself, love myself, and trust myself."*

Martha: *I am capable of taking care of myself loving myself and trusting myself.* [Opens her chest and extends her hands in front of her with both thumbs up with some hesitation, then places her hands over her heart and belly.]

Robert: *On the scale of a scale of zero to ten, how strongly do you experience resonance with that?*

Martha: *Five.*

Robert: *Right. So let us bring in some more resources. Let's get our red Siberian cat.* [Folds his arms in front of him as if holding something precious and begins to make a petting motion.] *Because we know that cat is capable. What would be that cat's message to you about this belief?*

Martha: [Mirrors the gesture.] *The cat is somehow letting me know that I am capable of taking care of myself. I just have to not lose track. It is not that I don't actually know how to take care of myself and love myself. I need to remember and make the space to do it.*

Robert: *Yes.*

Martha: *That I am capable of trusting myself and loving myself.* [Lengthens her spine, opens her chest and extends her hands in front of her with both thumbs up, then places her hands over her heart and belly. Smiles broadly.] *Now, it is like seven or eight.*

Robert: *Great. So now we are going to go to our next belief, which is that "I deserve it." Or, maybe better, that "I am worth taking care of." So let us connect that to that intention. Connect to yourself. Connect to the cat. Hold all three of those connections, make the statement and check for the resonance.*

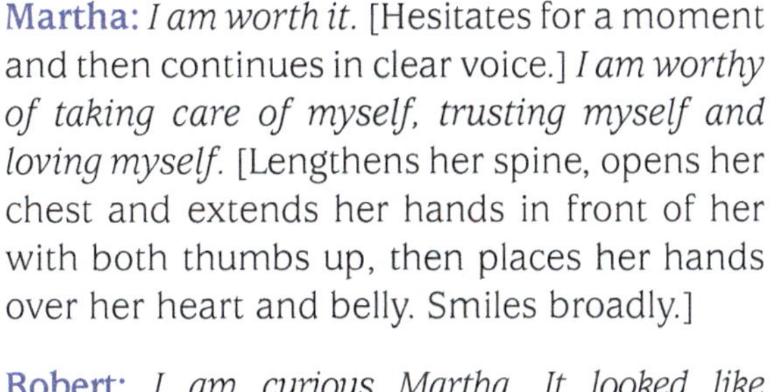

Martha: *I am worth it.* [Hesitates for a moment and then continues in clear voice.] *I am worthy of taking care of myself, trusting myself and loving myself.* [Lengthens her spine, opens her chest and extends her hands in front of her with both thumbs up, then places her hands over her heart and belly. Smiles broadly.]

Robert: *I am curious Martha. It looked like something really shifted for you just now. What happened?*

Martha: *I had some doubt at first and then I somehow got the message from the cat that, "You are at least as worthy as I am. I am just a cat and I am worth taking care of myself and loving myself. If I am, you are too." That brought the level way up.*

Robert: [Smiling] *That is some special cat. In fact, that brings us to our final belief, that "I have the permission and support to take care of myself, trust myself and love myself." If you connect to your intention, your center and this very special cat, and make that statement, how fully does that resonate?*

Martha: *I have the permission and support to take care of myself, trust myself and love myself.* [Lengthens her spine, opens her chest and extends her hands in front of her with both thumbs up, then places her hands over her heart and belly. Smiles broadly.] *With the cat here, I know for certain that I do. That cat is our everything.*

Putting the Six Beliefs Together

Robert: *Fantastic. Now, let us put that all together. Because this is where we are getting ready getting ready to move into action. So remember those three connections: your center, your intention, and your resource. And then we will say all of those beliefs together.*

"It is important and worth it. It is possible. It is appropriate. I am capable. I am worthy and I have the permission and support to take care of myself, trust myself and love myself." All right. So, I am ready when you are.

Martha: *It is really important for me to take care of myself and to trust myself and to love myself. It is possible and appropriate for me. And I know that I am capable of it. I have the permission and support, and I am worth it.* [Lengthens her spine, opens her chest and extends her hands in front of her with both thumbs up, then places her hands over her heart and belly. Starts to laugh.] *And, if you don't agree, go screw yourself!*

Robert: [Laughing] *I believe you! You are ready to move into action. By the way, this is where having an anchor and a practice can be important. For example, you may want to find images of the Siberian cat. And then I would put them in places where you most need to remember to take care of yourself. It could be at your office, your kitchen. So that you have that cat there to always remind you even if you consciously forget. You might also think of some practices that can help you.*

Martha: *I think it was important for me that there was a lot of petting. So I am ready to cover myself with cream and pat myself.*

Robert: *Is there a way to make sure that you have allocated time in your schedule to take care of yourself? Say something you would do every day? Is there something that you would do?*

Martha: *In the morning after the morning shower, I will cover myself in cream.* [Laughing] *I mean moisturizing cream not the kind of cream a cat drinks of course.*

Robert: [Smiling.] *I like the way that you say that.*

Martha: *There is also something about running. I live on the 17th floor and there is like a staircase. So, for me, there is something about running the stairs and feeling my strong legs.*

Robert: *Great. Now these are the kind of things we would go into more detail about in terms of planning and moving into action at Step 4. And I think you have a good start to work with here. So Martha, before we end, is there anything that you would want to share about what was helpful for you in terms of our interaction? Especially since we were doing it virtually.*

Martha: *I don't feel that it is distant. I do not feel that it is virtual. I can feel my connection with you.*

Robert: *What most helped you to have that sense of connection?*

Martha: *The experience of centeredness or feeling the center was really helpful. And I was able to reinstate this connection between you and me and me and myself. And I want to share something that was really surprising. I got used to treating my problems really seriously. And when this cat came as a resource it was really surprising. It was about something really simple and really down to earth like this cat. And it was fun. And it is something that is new for me.*

Robert: *Great.*

Martha: *Thank you so much.*

Strengthening the Generative State with Beliefs

GO THROUGH THE SIX
BELIEF STATEMENTS AND
DISCOVER IF THERE IS ONE
THAT BRINGS CRASH.

5) BRING IN YOUR
RESOURCES AND LET
THE LIMITING BELIEF
TRANSFORM.

6) ESTABLISH
PRACTICES TO
RECONNECT TO
YOUR INTENTION.

Summary

This particular *Generative Coaching* prototype involves adding a set of supporting beliefs to developing a generative state at **Step 3** in the coaching process. As always, we start in **COACH** State. And, especially when you are working virtually, using as much of the somatic mind as you can is very useful. You could hopefully get a sense in the demonstration with Martha of the value of having some active centering activities that you can do together with clients. And when you are coaching virtually you don't want to see the client on the screen, you want to kind of feel through the screen. Doing actions where you are mirroring each other really helps to make that stronger sense of connection and rapport.

In **Step 2** you are establishing the intention, and getting the simple statement, the image and the somatic model for that intention. Then, as you go to **Step 3**, you want to be sure that the client's connection to their intention is at least seven or more, and that their connection to their center is at least seven or more. Then you open to the resources. In the demonstration with Martha, it was really wonderful that she got this surprising image of the cat. That is how you really know that someone has developed good contact with their creative unconscious. Often our rational cognitive mind is trying to think, "Oh, it should be this or that person." But actually, when you open to the creative unconscious, you will have those lovely little surprises.

Once you have the intention, and you have the *three connections*, this is where you bring in these *six beliefs*. To work effectively with beliefs, you need to get some good reference experiences for what a strong, congruent belief is like. It is not about the content, it is about the level of resonance in the head, heart and gut. After you get those reference experiences you want to ground and anchor them with a somatic model for belief. As we observed in the demonstration with Martha, you will use this somatic model together with the belief statements to help check the level of resonance produced by each statement.

In this prototype, you use six simple belief statements: (1) "It is important. (2) It is possible. (3) It is appropriate. (4) I am capable. (5) I deserve it. (6) I have the permission and support." These are not long, complicated sentences to try to remember. They are very simple statements. And there is no magic in the words themselves. The magic is in the resonance. That is why, for each one of these statements, you are connecting with the somatic model for belief and checking the degree of resonance in the head, heart and gut.

Frequently, as we saw in the demonstration with Martha, instead of resonance you will get dissonance. When Martha attempted the belief statement "it is possible," she experienced this type of **CRASH** in her belly.

So what do we do?

The first thing, of course, is we recognize that this doubt is actually a valuable "team member." We say, "Welcome. I am sure it makes sense. Something here is needing to be heard or held or healed." Then, instead of becoming distracted or dissuaded, we go back and strengthen the three positive connections. So that doubt is there but, if we can welcome it and hold it and help the client connect more deeply to their center, stay connected to their intention, and especially to their resources, we can invoke the power and the magic of the generative state and the doubt becomes transformed. A key part of this prototype is getting support from the field of resources, usually in the form of some type of message from a role model or mentor that helps to strengthen positive resonance with the belief statement.

So, the simple pattern is, once you are at **Step 3** and you have the three positive connections, you help the client to find their connection to their reference experiences and somatic model to engage a strong, congruent belief. They say each belief out loud, make the gesture and check the degree of resonance in head, heart and gut. "It is important. It is possible. It is appropriate. I am capable. I deserve it. I have permission and support." If there is any dissonance or doubt, we welcome it, give it a place and then reconnect to the three positive connections, bringing in a message of support from the field of resources. This is frequently enough to transform the doubt. If not, you would need to shift to one of the **Step 5** prototypes for transforming obstacles (such as we will present later in this book).

When the three positive connections are strong and supported by the six key beliefs, the client will naturally start shifting to **Step 4**. and be ready to move into action, as we could see at the end of the demonstration with Martha. And that is where we will go next.

Being a Person

Be a person here. Stand by the river,
invoke the owls. Invoke winter, then spring.
Let any season that wants to come here make its own call.
After that sound goes away, wait.

A slow bubble rises through the earth
and begins to include sky, stars, all space,
even the outracing, expanding thought.
Come back and hear the little sound again.

Suddenly this dream you are having matches
everyone's dream, and the result is the world.
If a different call came there wouldn't be any
world, or you, or the river, or the owls calling.

How you stand here is important. How you
listen for the next things to happen. How you breathe.

— William Stafford

Chapter 5

Step 4
Moving Into Action

In this chapter we will be going more deeply into **Step 4** of the *Generative Coaching* process, which is about moving into action. This step is about shifting from Dreamer to Realist and involves the delicate dance between the quantum field of possibilities and the world of classical reality. You can hear some of the dynamics of this dance in the poem *Being a Person* by the late American poet William Stafford. The poem describes a movement of awareness out to the "sky, stars, all space" and then back again to the "little sound." It also talks about the importance of the resonance of our dreams with those of others in creating reality, and emphasizes that the way we stand, listen, and breathe are part of the way that we create our realities. These are all key issues that we will be addressing in this chapter.

Chunking

This dynamic movement between the quantum field and classical reality is what we have referred to in our previous volumes as "chunking." The process of chunking involves breaking something down into its component parts. Chunking up has to do with assembling and integrating pieces into successively larger wholes—such as letters into words into sentences into paragraphs into chapters, etc. Moving into action is essentially about chunking the intention down into specific action steps; what we have referred to in previous volumes as a "storyboard."

Effectively moving into action actually involves being able to move in both directions—chunking down and chunking up. Just like composing a song, writing a book, or preparing a meal, there are times when we need to break things down into smaller chunks and other times when we need to assemble them into larger chunks in order make our creation.

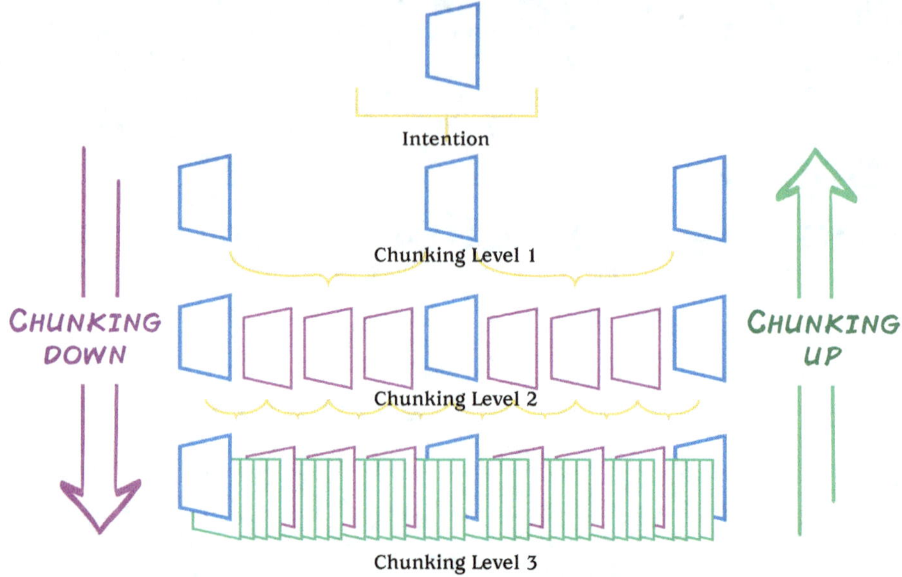

Moving into action involves chunking down the intention into specific steps.

Connecting and Managing Different Levels of Change

One of the roadmaps that we use to guide this process in generative change work is based on the work of one of our main mutual mentors Gregory Bateson. Bateson formulated the notion of *different levels of learning* to describe the natural need of all creatures to be able to chunk up and down while acquiring new behaviors. According to this model, specific behaviors form classes, and classes of behavior in turn form systems of those classes; and vice versa.

Robert has adapted Bateson's levels of learning into a particular map that can be really helpful known as *NeuroLogical Levels* or simply *Levels of Learning and Change* (see *From Coach to Awakener*, 2003). According to the model, the *environment* level involves the specific external conditions in which our behavior takes place. *Behaviors* without any inner map, plan or strategy to guide them, however, are like knee jerk reactions, habits or rituals. At the level of *capability*, we are able to select, alter and adapt a class of behaviors to a wider set of external situations. At the level of *beliefs and values* we may encourage, inhibit, or generalize a particular strategy, plan, or way of thinking. *Identity*, of course, consolidates whole systems of beliefs and values into a sense of self. While each level becomes more abstracted from the specifics of behavior and sensory experience, it actually has more and more widespread effect on our behavior and experience. The level of *purpose* acknowledges the fact that we are a part of a larger "holon" that reaches beyond ourselves as individuals to our family, community, and global systems.

There is an old saying that "purpose directs activity." We see this in our Generative Coaching work, as we frequently find that intentions are set at the level of purpose and identity. This is a natural consequence of the question we typically ask at Step 2 of the coaching process, "What do you most want to create or become in the world?

In the previous chapter, we introduced the role of beliefs as a key part of the generative state. As the *Levels* map illustrates, beliefs and their related values become a key part of helping to chunk the intention down, especially those related to our capabilities and actions, which is our main focus at Step 4. We are seeking to help the coachee define what capabilities they need and which sequence of actions to take in order to express their intention in a particular environmental context. We are moving from purpose into action.

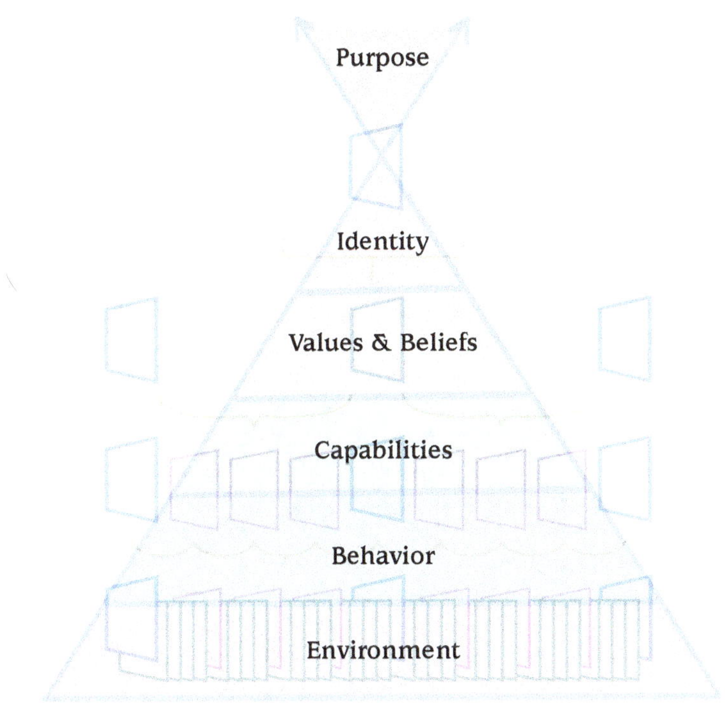

**The various levels of learning and change
define different "chunk sizes" of our experience.**

Ego and Soul

Another dynamic that we can important when mapping the path from purpose to action is that between the complementary aspects of our lives we call "ego" and "soul." According to psychoanalysis, the *ego* is "the part of the psyche that mediates between the conscious and the unconscious and is responsible for reality testing and a sense of personal identity." Thus, the ego has to do with the development and preservation of our sense of a separate self, perceiving reality from its own individual perspective.

At the level of environment, the ego tends to focus on dangers and constraints, and the pursuit of short-term gain and pleasure. Consequently, at the level of behavior, the ego tends to be more reactive to external conditions. The capabilities associated with the ego are generally those connected with the cognitive intellect such as analysis and strategy. At the level of beliefs and values the ego focuses on safety, security, approval, control, achievement and self-benefit. At the identity level, ego relates to our social roles and who we feel we should be or need to be. At the level of purpose our ego is oriented toward survival, recognition and ambition.

From the perspective of generative change, the ego can be considered a cognitively constructed map or model of one's "self" and as a natural developmental process. These notions of "reality" and "self" associated with the ego, however, are influenced by external references such as social norms, cultural values and family patterns. Like all maps or models, it is necessarily shaped by the processes of deletion, distortion and generalization. When these distortions create too much separation from the actual territory and potential of ourselves they can create symptoms. Some characteristics of an unhealthy ego take the form of either self-inflation (i.e.,pride, arrogance, self-importance, narcissism and self-infatuation) or self-depreciation (i.e., self-judgment, depression, self-criticism, lack of self-worth and self-confidence, etc.). These can lead us to become overly gripped by greed, fear and survival strategies (fight, flight, freeze).

The *soul* is our unique life force, essence or energy that we come into the world with and that comes into the world through us. As a newborn baby, for instance, we do not yet have an ego, but we have a unique energy and being that is the foundation for our identity. This energy is expressed through our bodies and our interface with the larger fields surrounding us. Because the soul is an energetic "deep structure," it is not associated with any particular content—and therefore is not constructed from influences such as society, culture and family. It does, however, express itself in the form of contribution to these as larger fields. Thus, rather than being an objectified or separate self, the soul is our expression of an unfolding, connected self.

At the level of environment, the soul tends to focus on opportunities for expression and growth. As a result, at the level of behavior, the soul tends to respond more proactively to external conditions. The capabilities associated with the soul are generally those related to the perception and management of energy and emotional intelligence. At the level of beliefs and values, the soul focuses on internal motivations such as service, contribution, connection, being, expansion and awakening. At the identity level, soul relates to our mission and the unique gifts that we bring into the world. At the level of purpose, the soul is oriented toward our vision of what we want to create in the world through us but that is beyond us.

Clearly, both of these aspects of ourselves are necessary for a healthy and successful existence. The primary questions with respect to the soul are those related to vision and mission: "What do I want to create in the world through me that is beyond me?" and "What is my unique contribution to bringing that vision into expression?" The questions relating to our ego are, "What type of life do I want to create for myself?" and "What type of person do I need to be in order to create the life I want?"

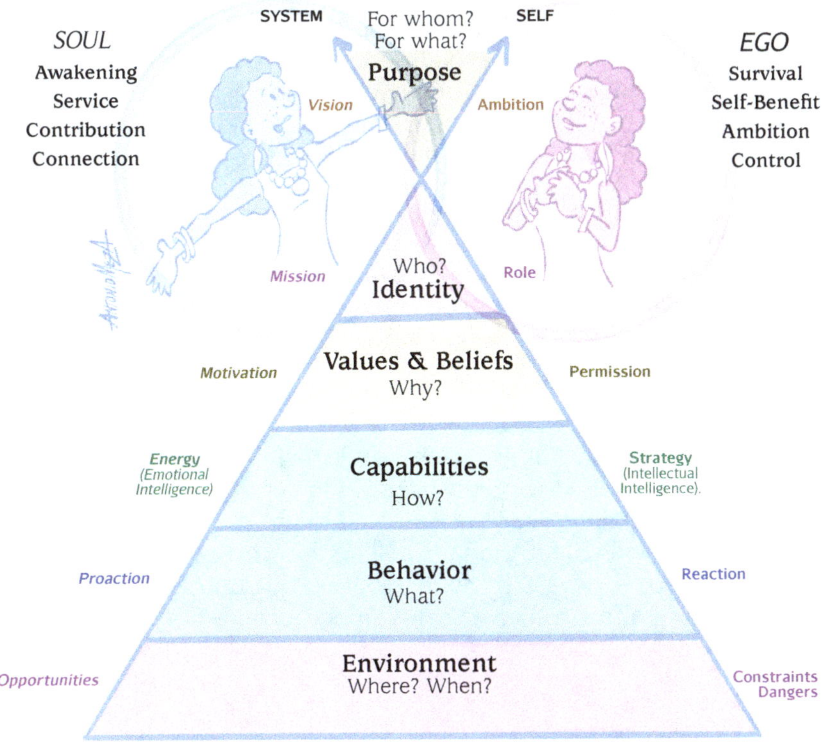

**The various levels of change may be engaged
in support of either our ego or soul**

When our body (somatic mind) and our intellect (cognitive mind) connect like two dancers responding to the music of life, then our soul has a vehicle for expression and we find ourselves more alive, with greater joy, heightened intuition and more at home in the world. Charisma, passion and presence emerge naturally when these two forces (ego and soul; ambition and vision) are aligned. Optimum performance comes when the ego is in service of the soul. When we "sell our soul" for ego benefits, we may have short-term success but are heading for a crisis in the long run.

Balancing Ego and Soul

It is important to keep in mind that we need both of these complementary aspects of ourselves to achieve sustainable survival and growth. Consider, for example, that generative change, and the need for generative change, often starts at the environmental level. On a global scale, pandemics, wars, climate catastrophes, and the consequent economic crises, bring about danger and impose lots of constraints. But such disruptions also create opportunities. And we can take advantage of these opportunities and maybe even create new opportunities.

And to do that, we need to go to our actions, our behaviors. So, we have to react to the constraints and the dangers, but we also have to proactively take advantage of the opportunities. How do we know what to do? How do we know which behaviors and which reactions to have and which proactive actions to take? Clearly, the actions that we take come from which capabilities we have. That has to do with this level of *how* we decide.

Of course, to react effectively, we need to have some kind of cognitive intelligence, some kind of strategic plan. But also, to take the right actions, we need to have some kind of emotional intelligence as well in order to activate the energy we are going to need to execute the plan.

As an example, as coaches, reflect on switching from doing coaching in person to doing coaching virtually (and vice versa). You will need to activate and sometimes develop certain capabilities. Some are technical capabilities, such as learning to use particular technology. But others will involve emotional intelligence. You need to learn how, when you can't be physically with somebody, you can still establish that same sense of a strong human connection.

So, changes in "where and when" we are, changes in our outer world, require us to be generative in our behavior, our actions and "what" we do. But that also then requires us to be generative in how we do what we do—to develop new competencies and new capabilities.

And then, this is where belief comes in. Because *how* we do things and *what* we do is a function of why we are doing it. And this level of why has to do with our motivation. This is this level of belief and also our values. Now, we put beliefs and values at the same level because the most impactful beliefs that we have are connected to our core values. Meaning, the reason I would believe something is important or is worth it is because that something is connected to my values. So, again, we see that beliefs play a very pivotal role in determining whether we use capabilities, whether we develop certain capabilities, and where we put our energy and our attention.

But we are certainly something more than our beliefs. We are not just the sum total of our beliefs. When I say there's an "I" who believes something, this I that believes it is not the belief. So, we would say this "I" is a deeper identity that is beyond the programming. And this identity expresses itself in terms of both a "role" and a "mission."

A *role* would be something like choosing to be a "generative coach." It involves the question, "What is the role I take with respect to others in the world?" In the demonstration with James in Chapter 3, he said, "I realized that I'd always worked in businesses and for other people before. But that role doesn't really fit who I deeply am. That's why I started my own business. That's why I took this different role."

This identity is also about why we change roles; because what I have to contribute and what I have to bring to the world is also a part of the sense of living my life—not just what somebody else expects from me. That is what we would call your *"mission,"* which is, "What is it that you are bringing to the world through you?" This relates to things that are beyond you that you are in service of. And that's our sense of purpose—for whom, for what else am I here to contribute, to serve, to give?

In fulfilling our purpose, we have this very interesting interaction between the bigger system and our self. At this highest level, we have the dynamic between vision and ambition. Our vision has to do with "what I want to create in the world through me that is beyond me." Our ambitions typically relate to "what type of life I want to create for myself." This is often one of the most challenging places that people find to bring that sense of balance to. And we saw it very clearly in the demonstration with Martha. She said, "Right now, I'm giving so much to others. I'm doing so much for other people." She was being really called to give a lot on the vision and mission side; to give to others, to give to the system. The imbalance was, "I'm not taking care of myself." So, she was really needing to bring her identity and purpose back into balance.

This is where we get back to this important notion of the holon. If I am part of this bigger holon, I have to take care of me in order to be able to continue to care for something bigger than me. If I am only taking care of others, and I become sick or incapacitated, then I am not very much good to anybody. At the same time, and again this is what we could see in the demo with James, "I have my contribution to make." And that is an equally powerful drive.

So, if we go out of balance on one side, we become this kind of altruistic person who has lost themselves. And it is frankly not sustainable to do that. On the other side, you have the narcissist, the person who only thinks of themselves, only is concerned with their ego needs. And that is not sustainable either. If you recall those five regrets of the dying, some were about, "I didn't take care of myself." Others were, "I didn't keep connection with others."

What we want to do from a generative coaching perspective is to make sure that our coachees stay aligned and balanced as they take action toward their intention. So, what we will do in the next prototype is to begin to move from vision into action and from Dreamer into Realist in a balanced way. And as we do that, we are going to be also more than likely getting ready to meet some of the Critic as well.

In our next practice, we're going to be working with the *Levels of Change* pyramid in two stages. First is getting clarity about the way an intention would be expressed with respect to the highest levels – the levels of vision, mission, ambition, and role. And this all revolves around this deep inner sense of what comes from our center, which is what we're going to call our passion. The second stage is to align the other levels of the pyramid to support these expressions of the intention.

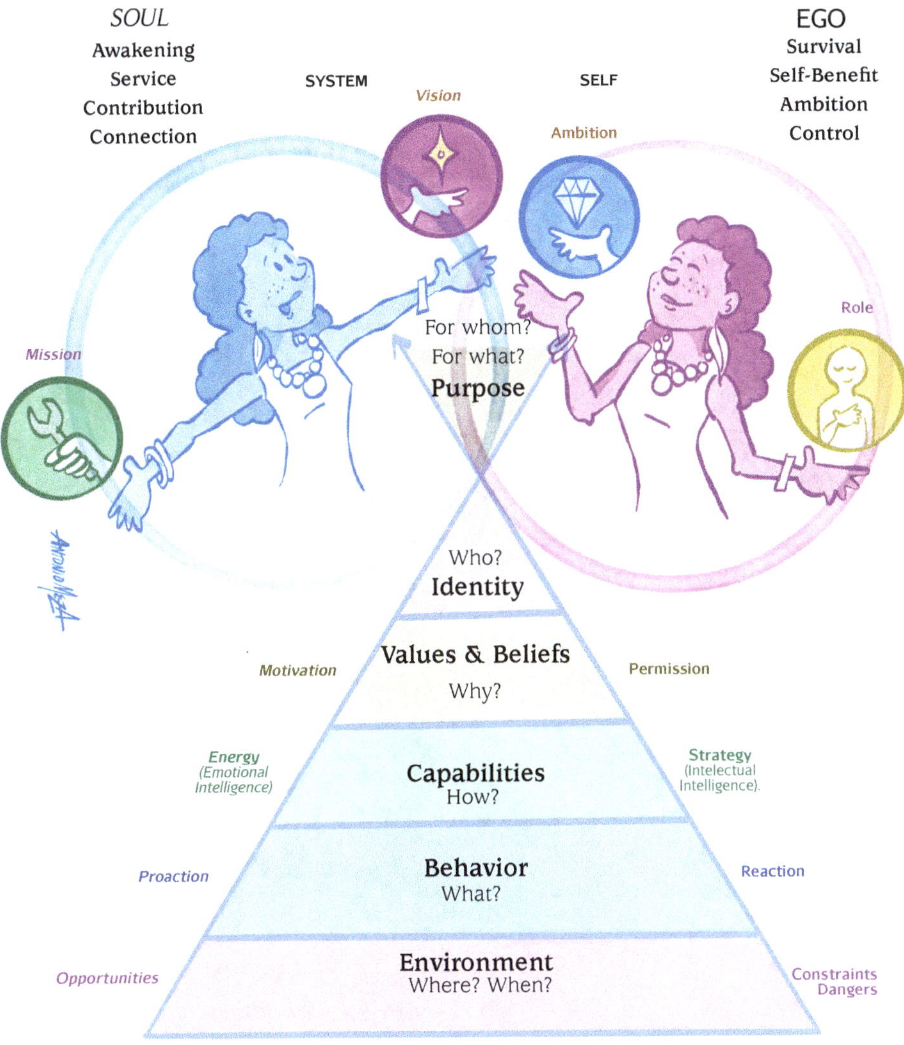

**Getting a good balance at the higher levels of change
makes it easier to balance and align the lower levels.**

Stage 1: Chunking Down Intention–Moving from Dreamer to Realist

So, initially, we are going to be working with this combination of five questions that are important and profound explorations having to do with your coachee's intention. Incidentally, those of you who do work with businesses or even have your own business, these questions can be asked not only just about you as an individual, but can also be asked in regard to a team or organization.

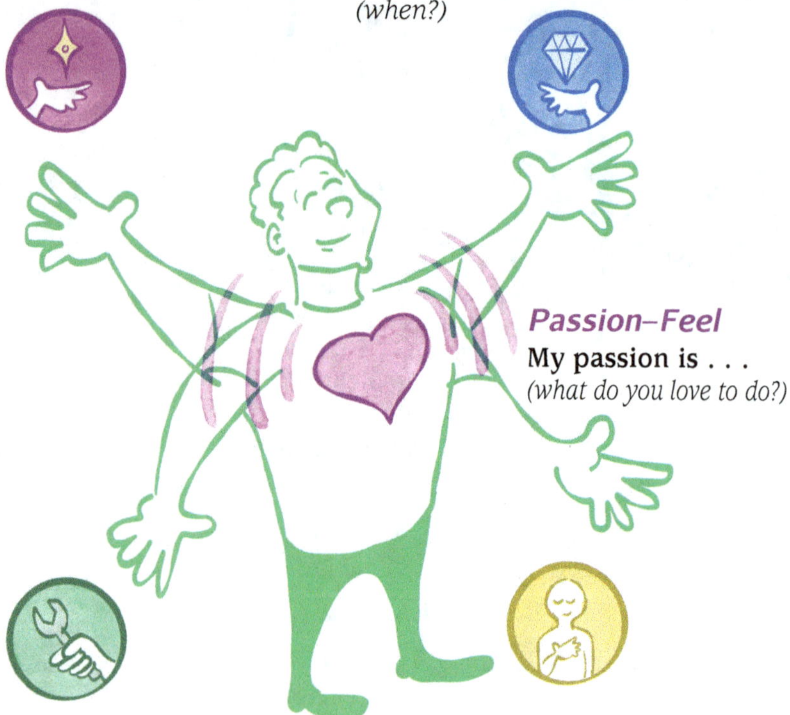

Five clarifying questions for chunking down intention

At the center of this exploration is this question, "What is your *passion*? What is it that you love to do? Where does your energy come from?" I can guarantee you that you cannot be generative if you have no passion. Warren Buffett, who is always in the top five wealthiest people on the planet, says it very simply. He says, "If you have no passion, you have no energy. If you have no energy, you have nothing." No passion, no energy. No energy, nothing. Very often our center is a source for our passion, especially when we can connect our belly center to our heart center. So, this is our starting question.

Then from that passion, we look to the future and see what is possible through the filter of our passion. And this is what forms our *vision*. "What is possible in the future? What is the future I would like to see? What will be better or different? What would there be more of? What would there be less of?" Now, that vision can be for any part of the holon. It can be for yourself, it can be for your family, it can be for your profession, or can be for our world. Very often, that's going to be determined by what is happening in the circumstances around us.

When we connect our passion to our vision, we naturally want to begin to do something, and that is where we start to move from the Dreamer to the Realist. This is where we are going to begin moving into action. And this is what we are calling your *mission* with respect to that particular vision. The question here is, "What is it that you are going to do in order to get what result? What will you be doing for whom and for what purpose? What is unique or special about what you will do?" And that is where we are going to start to get the first sense of a kind of storyboard.

Then we go to what we call the *ambition*. We *feel* our *passion*, we see the possibilities through our *vision* and we begin to *take action* with our *mission*. And through those actions we aim to *achieve* specific goals. And this is what we are calling *ambition*. "What do you want to achieve concretely? By when?" Ambition engages the Realist mentality even more. The specific goals associated with our ambitions need to be quantifiable and reached within specific time frame. Big goals may be set for two to five years, but some key ambitions could be two to five months or two to five weeks, given the degree of change and uncertainties of the situation.

And then that final question there is about *role* and who you will *become* if you succeed in your ambition. "In order to achieve your ambition, who do you need to become? Who will you become if you achieve it? How will your role expand or grow? What more of your potential will be expressed?" It is not always easy or appropriate to answer this question in a literal way, so we will often ask coachees to express this using an example or metaphor.

Now all of these different dimensions of our intention are interconnected and, when balanced and aligned, they support each other. Role, for instance, is connected to ambition. There is a really key connection between your ambition, your achievements, and your role. For example, if I achieve writing a book, I become an author. And to become an author I have to write something. If I say to somebody, "I'm an author" and they ask, "What have you written?" and I say, "Well, I haven't written anything," it wouldn't make any sense. Similarly, if I start a business, I become an entrepreneur. If I don't start a business, I'm not an entrepreneur. So again, there is an important connection between achievements and our role.

But there is also a key connection between role and mission. In the demonstration with Kate in Chapter 2, she initially said, "I really want to step into this role of Generative Coach and put myself out there. But I have this fear." That shifted, however, when she was able to connect to her center and sense of mission that "I can do something to help others." Connecting role and mission creates a powerful congruence and motivation at the identity level.

It is often very useful to clarify and connect these various dimensions of intention when moving into action, since usually only one of them is expressed when a coachee is stating his or her intention. For example, when you ask people, "What do you most want to create?" Sometimes they answer in terms of a vision, "I want to see my family be happier." Other times, they answer in terms of a role and say, "I want to become X." Other times, they answer in terms of an ambition such as, "I want to make X amount of money." Sometimes they answer in terms of a mission, "I want to help people heal." So, this exploration helps to fill out how these all relate to one another at the top of the pyramid.

Bringing In a Timeline to Create a Compelling Future

The way we are going to work with these in this practice is to put them on a timeline. This is what we call creating a compelling future. And we are going to start in the present with the feeling of passion. Then, when we take that passion and bring it up the timeline to the future, we are engaging the **Dreamer** to create a vision.

Then we say, "Okay, what are you going to do from your passion to reach that dream?" And that is when we begin to engage the **Realist**.

And then the other **Realist** questions are, "Through doing that, what do you want to achieve that is bringing you closer to the vision?" And then, "Who do you become or need to become in order to achieve that?"

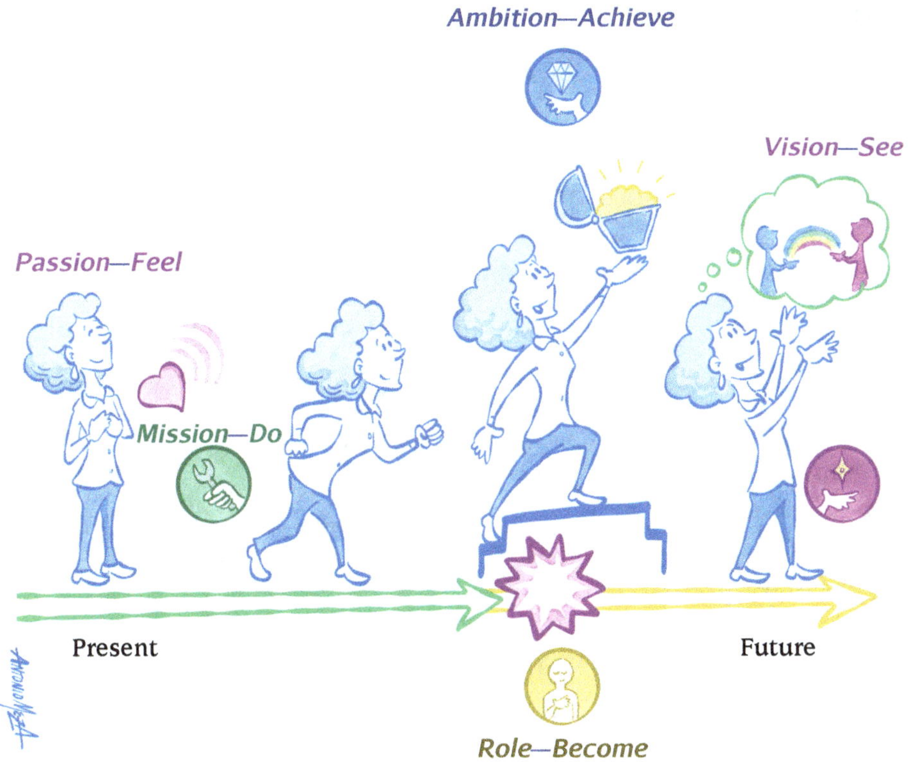

So again, we have our passion in the present. When we project that into the future, we can begin to see other possibilities. When we put that passion into action and service of our vision, it becomes a mission, and we start moving to **Realist**. And then, as we act, we begin to achieve concrete results. That's our ambition. And through achieving and in order to achieve it, we evolve our role.

Demonstration of Creating a Compelling Future

The following is a transcript of a demonstration of *Creating a Compelling Future* that Robert did as part of a virtual training course.

Alice: *Nice to meet you. My name is Alice.*

Robert: *Wonderful to meet you, Alice. I'm looking forward to this exploration with you. Now, Alice, to do this, it's going to be best to have a little bit of a timeline. We're going to need enough room that we can take three steps.*

Alice: *I have space for three steps.*

Robert: *Let's just practice. Let's take one. Two. Three. And make sure we're still in the picture.* [Robert and Alice take a few steps together.] *Okay, so now, let's go back to the present.* [Robert and Alice take a few steps back.] *And of course, first thing we want to do is come into our COACH State. So, what is one of your good ways to come into your COACH State?*

Alice: *I have this way of doing things, it might be a bit strange, but I just imagine a specific song. I rehearse it in my head and then I dance to it.* [Begins to dance. Smiles broadly.]

Robert: [Mirrors Alice's movements. Smiles.] *I don't know the song, but I like the dance. It's beautiful. It feels to me it has both strength and flexibility and a little bit of playfulness.*

Alice: *And I can feel my center while dancing. I feel it really well.*

Robert: *That's great. So, Alice, as you do that now, what would you say is your level of your COACH State? Zero to ten.*

Alice: *Eight.*

Robert: *Eight, good. Yeah, I can see it looks like a solid eight. So, Alice, what we're going to do to find the intention is we're going to do something a little bit different than we've done in other practices, which is to start with not only your center but also your passion. The question for finding your passion is, "What is it that gives you energy?" Now, here's the thing, it's not about any particular action. It's about what that brings to you. For example, I'll share with you my five words and my gestures for my passion.*

I have a passion for **connection**; *I like connecting with people, I like connecting ideas, I like connecting things together. And this is my gesture . . .* [Interlaces his fingers.] *And my second word and gesture are about* **awakening**. [Lifts his hands over his head as if tracing two halves of a rainbow.] *It is about being aware of our place in a bigger holon. And my third word and my third for my passion is* **creativity**, *and this is my gesture for that.* [Makes a revolving gesture with both hands in front of him.] *I like to create things, create seminars, create books, create music, create drawings, etc. Then, my fourth word and my fourth gesture are* **contribution**. [Gestures out from his body as if offering something with his hands.] *I like to contribute to people. And my fifth word and my fifth gesture is* **inspiration**. [Extends his arms and hands in front of him and lifts them upward in an encouraging gesture.]

So that would be an example of what we mean by passion. It's not about specific things. It's about these words that I know I can express them in many ways. So, for you, Alice, if you really tuned into what you get excited about, what you love to do, what brings you energy. What would be your first word and your first gesture?

Alice: *I love to bring to people something that I can call a belief in* **uniqueness**. *A way to believe in something unique.* [Brings her palms together in front of her and opens her fingers like a flower blossoming.] *And that's my movement.*

Robert: [Mirrors the gesture.] *Yeah. So, this passion for this belief in uniqueness. What would be your second word and your second gesture?*

Alice: *I like to* **inspire**. [Lifts both hands above her shoulders, wiggles her fingers and smiles.]

Robert: *I like that, too.* [Mirrors the gesture.] *I like to inspire people too. So, this first one is uniqueness, belief in uniqueness.* [Opens fingers in front of him like a flower blossoming.] *And then inspire.* [Lifts hands above shoulders and wiggles fingers.] *And again, we can see the whole idea here of why we connect to our passion is to get energy. What would be your third word and your third gesture?*

Alice: *I somehow get this word of* **transformation**.

Robert: *Transformation, yeah.*

Alice: *Yeah, the transformation of the personality.* [Brings hands to heart and then opens them out from the body.]

Robert: [Mirrors gesture.] *I love it. Great. So, we have uniqueness. Inspiration. Transformation.* [Makes the gesture for each.] *Fantastic. What would be your fourth word and your fourth gesture?*

Alice: *It's* **realization** *or understanding realization.* [Moves hands downward from head to belly.]

Robert: *Understanding realization.* [Mirrors the gesture.]

Alice: *Yes.*

Robert: *Fantastic. And I feel a lot of resonance to you with these passions. So, uniqueness. Inspiration. Transformation. And realization.* [Makes the gesture for each.] *All right. What about the final word, the fifth word and fifth gesture?*

Alice: *Activity, activity, something like that, activity.* [Moves arms and upper body in a rotating motion.]

Robert: [Mirrors gesture.] *Perfect. Great. And again, we can see that each of these naturally brings greater energy to you. So, let's put them all together. Uniqueness. Inspiration. Transformation. Realization. And activity.* [Makes the gesture for each.]

Alice: [Repeats the gestures and smiles broadly.]

Robert: *Great. So now, just really tune into not only that sense of your center, but that quality of aliveness and energy that comes from connecting to your passion. And to set our intention, the question would be, "Where would you like to have or see more of these qualities either in your life or in what you do for others?" It could be in your profession, in your relationship or in your own personal activity.*

Alice: *In my profession and in the nearest future, I want to create an online training about how to expand your capabilities and how to find something that you want to create in your life.*

Robert: *Wow, that sounds great. This is actually a perfect exercise for that. So, we're going to take three steps to the future. You're going to bring your passion. And bring it to that project. So, when we're ready, we're going to take those three steps to the dream. One. Two. Three.* [Robert and Alice take a few steps together.]

And really put yourself into this place where you say, okay, this is what I want to create through this online program. And as you're here in the future, remember your passion. So, the words and gestures—Uniqueness, Inspiration. Transformation. Realization. Activity. [Robert and Alice make the gestures for each word.] *As you bring that energy of that passion to your profession and to your project, what is your vision? What do you see that could be possible? And this is really that question of, what would you want to create?*

Alice: *I see people who are happily going to work and wake up every morning with this feeling like, "Yay! Finally, I get to work!"*

Robert: *Beautiful, that's a beautiful vision. What would be your gesture?*

Alice: *Like this.* [Puts one foot forward, extends her arms in front of her and smiles.]

Robert: [Mirrors the gesture.] *Great. So again, this is the idea that the intention begins with a vision of people really coming to work with their passion. You have a great example of vision because you actually see it. You see these people. So that's the dream. Now we're going to take three steps back to the present.* [Robert and Alice take a few steps back.] *Now, as you see the future, you can see that vision for your project. And you can feel your passion. Maybe even connect to those gestures and those words again. Belief in uniqueness. Inspiration. Transformation. Realization. And activity.* [Robert and Alice make the gestures for each word.]

As you feel your passion and connect to that vision of your intention, what resources will you need? Who or what from your field of resources can support you?

Alice: *What comes to me is a river. There is a river near where I live that I often go to for inspiration. It is constantly flowing but has clear boarders that contain the movement.*

Robert: *Wow. Great. As you connect to that river, to your passion and to your vision for your project, we're going to take one step forward and explore the questions, "What are you going to do to help create that vision? What is your action? What is your mission? What is your contribution to this vision? What do you do?"*

Alice: *First of all, I have to cope with my inner fear, because I kind of sense some little person inside of me who is saying, "It's too early. It's too early to do that."*

Robert: *So, first of all, we want to say to this part, "Welcome. I'm sure it makes sense." And obviously, something there is really wanting to be heard, to be held. So, we can say "welcome" to that.*

Alice: *Welcome.*

Robert: *And, as you do, also stay connected to your passion, to your vision and to that river that is constantly flowing within those clear boundaries. As you do, you can wonder, "What resource does this little part need?"*

Alice: *It maybe would be a daily plan of actions, a daily action plan.*

Robert: *Actually, out of curiosity, what would having that daily action plan give her? Would she then feel more confident or have more clarity?*

Alice: *It would give me more of a systematic approach. Because I am quite a creative and artistic person, and for me, it's quite hard to kind of pack myself up and put myself in a box.*

Robert: *So, I think what becomes interesting here is that this little part of you is actually one of your team members. So instead of being an obstacle, it's actually the one that helps you remember to create a daily action plan. In order to reach that vision and to do your mission, you're going to need a little bit more structure. This part helps you be a better Realist and not just a Dreamer. So, what would be your gesture for that? Putting things in order, having that plan.*

Alice: *It's something like that.* [Moves hands out from her body alternating one hand in front of the other as if marking different steps.] *That's what comes.*

Robert: *Yeah.* [Mirrors the gesture.] *So that's very important to realize and notice. At first, it seems like, oh, it's an obstacle, that's my fear. But actually, when we can hold that fear from a generative state, it turns out, "Oh, actually, she's really a resource for me."*

Alice: *And it also resembles this movement of a transformation.* [Brings hands to heart and then opens them out from the body.]

Robert: *That's very interesting, isn't it?*

Alice: *Yeah, that's interesting.*

Robert: *So now, let's find out what happens if you do that; if you can have that structure, and your passion and your vision and your river. Let's take another step forward. If you do that, what will you achieve? What is your ambition? What do you want to achieve? And let's look at a certain timeframe. Would it be in six months? What will you achieve if you do this?*

Alice: *I get this notion of five months.*

Robert: *And what will you concretely accomplish in those five months?*

Alice: In five months, I'll have the clear and distinct program, and I'll also close all the educational courses that I'm a part of today.

Robert: Wow. Okay. So now really put yourself in that accomplishment. [Robert and Alice take a step together.] *I've got my program clear. I've cleared away the other things. And if you can really see that, hear that and feel that, what is your gesture for achieving that?*

Alice: I want to do something like that. [Pumps her fists and raises her arms triumphantly above her head.] *Yes!* [Smiles broadly.]

Robert: Okay. [Mirrors gesture. Smiles.] *So now, the last exploration here is, if you do that, if you achieve that, who have you become or become more of? What is your new role? What is this new you?*

Alice: My new role would be someone who transforms the personality, I would say.

Robert: Actually, this is where sometimes a symbol, or an image can be really helpful. The symbol might be a butterfly coming out of a cocoon or something. What would be your image or your symbol for this role?

Alice: Can it be a gesture?

Robert: Yeah, sure.

Alice: I don't know why but I wanted to kind of crouch, to sit down, like a baby who is still in her mother's belly, who is connected to herself to all the parts, and she is herself. [Leans forward and wraps her arms around herself.]

Robert: Wow. So, you are becoming this person who is bringing transformation of personality. [Mirrors the gesture.] *Great.*

Alice: [Repeats the gesture.] *Yeah.*

Robert: *And becoming this will lead you to the next step.* [Robert and Alice take a step together.] *We step into that vision. And, remembering your gesture for that vision, which was . . .*

Alice: [Puts one foot forward, extends her arms in front of her and smiles broadly.] *And now I can see happy people. I have helped them to change their vision.*

Robert: *Yes.*

Alice: *I want to share that, in 2014, I went through a successful healing process with breast cancer. And when people ask me, how I did that, I always answer that it's not how you do the things; it's about transforming your consciousness. And I really performed a great deal of work transforming my own consciousness.*

Robert: *Thank you for sharing that. That touches me. And I think sometimes it's meeting those challenges that show us our mission. They certainly are a powerful reference experience, So, connecting to that experience, what I'd like to do,*

1) **GET INTO A GENERATIVE STATE.** 2) **FIND RESOURCES.** 3) **SET YOUR INTENTION— YOUR VISION.**

Alice, is walk again through the whole storyboard. Let's take three steps back. [Robert and Alice take three steps back together.] *In the present, we start in our COACH state.* [Robert begins to dance. Alice joins him and they both smile.] *Then we connect to the passion. Which is uniqueness. Inspiration. Transformation. Realization. Activity.* [Robert and Alice make the gestures for each word.] *And we connect to your vision of happy people at work and to your resource of the river.*

And then we take that step into organizing that passion by creating daily plans of actions for five months . . . [Moves hands out from his body alternating one hand in front of the other. Alice makes the same gesture.] *We take another step, and you have your program and you have cleared your schedule.* [Pumps his fists and raises his arms triumphantly above his head. Alice mirrors the gesture and smiles broadly.] *And you become this new role.* [Leans forward and wraps his arms around himself. Alice mirrors the gesture, continuing to smile broadly.] *And that allows you to take that next step into the vision.* [Puts one foot forward and extends and his arms in front of him. Alice mirrors the gesture and smiles broadly.]

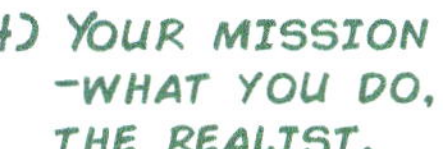

This is the big storyboard. There are still a lot of details to fill in. But now you have a path. So, let's take our three steps back to the beginning. [Robert and Alice take three steps back together.] *And as you look at that path in front of you, let's end by bringing in those six beliefs. Do you have a reference experience and a gesture for believing something strongly and congruently?*

Alice: *Oh yes. Absolutely. It is my healing process with breast cancer and knowing that I can truly transform myself.* [Places both hands over her diaphragm and nods her head.]

Robert: [Mirrors the gesture.] *Great. I am sure that is a profound reference experience. So, as you look up your timeline and see your vision, the first belief is that "this is important and it's worth it." Can you say that out loud with your gesture?*

Alice: *It's important.* [Places both hands over her diaphragm and nods her head.]

Robert: *And it's possible.*

Alice: *That is possible.* [Makes her gesture for belief.]

Robert: *And, as you look at that storyboard we've just created, it is appropriate. This will work."*

Alice: *It is appropriate, and my plan will work.* [Makes her gesture for belief.]

Robert: *Yes. And I'm capable to do it.*

Alice: *I am capable.* [Makes her gesture for belief.]

Robert: *And then the next one is that I'm worthy, I'm worth it.*

Alice: *I'm worth it. I'm worth it. Yes.* [Makes her gesture for belief.]

Robert: *And finally, I have the permission and support to do it.*

Alice: *I really believe that I have the permission and support.* [Makes her gesture for belief. Smiles broadly.] *And I totally will do it.*

Robert: *I believe you! Our last step is to put all these beliefs together. It is important. It is possible. It is appropriate. I am capable. I deserve it. I have the permission and support. And I can do it. This will work. This will bring me to here.* [Robert and Alice take three steps forward.]

Alice: *Finally, I did it.* [Pumps her fists and raises her arms triumphantly, smiling broadly.]

Robert: *I am sure you will, and I send you my full support for your path. And thank you for sharing your own story of healing and transformation.*

Alice: *I'm really glad to work with you. I got a lot of new realizations. And what I realized, what I understood, is that it is totally real, and I just have to take steps.*

Robert: *Yes, yes, that's beautiful. So, Alice, the last question is, is there anything that you can share about what was helpful, especially in this virtual environment?*

Alice: *For me, it was quite unusual to be in a coachee role. Especially working with you. And when they told me that I would be a client of yours, I was just crying with tears of happiness. And I'll keep this day in my stash of resourceful days that will help me to achieve my intentions.*

Robert: *Yes, I feel that. And I just want to finish by saying you are definitely worth it.*

Alice: *And hugs, virtual hugs.*

Summary

To summarize the prototype, we're working with a physical timeline that uses three symbolic steps to the future. We start in the present with COACH State and then connect to our passion. We then find those five words and gestures that bring us a sense of energy and motivation. Next, we define intention. In Alice's case, it was about creating an online platform to help people make a transformation of their identity.

Next, we want to get the vision for that intention. And that's where we connect with the passion and take the three steps forward into the future. Now, what's important is that you're dreaming from the passion. It's not just an intellectual idea. And Alice gave us a really great example of a vision. She said, "I can see people having the sense of loving to go into work."

Then you are taking the three steps back to the present and developing a generative state by connecting to a resource from your field of resources, which will support you to reach the vision. Next, we say, "Okay, I see the vision, I connect to the passion and my resources, and I move into action." Now interestingly, when Alice did that, at first it kind of looked like there was an obstacle. She said, "I have to get beyond this fear." But notice how, once we were able to welcome that fear and hold that fear, it had a very positive intention. In fact, it was an important team member. And, when we could hold this fear and bring resources to it in a generative state, it turned into this action of bringing structure. Of course, we don't always meet a seeming obstacle at that step. Often, the steps begin to come easily and naturally.

Either way, it leads us to the next step. "If I do that, what do I want to achieve or accomplish?" And here is where it is important to be concrete. In Alice's case, she said, "I'll have my own program in place. I'll have cleared away these other obligations." As with the previous steps, we get our gesture for that, and then we ask, "If you achieve that, how have you expanded your role? What is the bigger you that you have become?" And it is useful to get a symbol and, of course, a gesture for that. You then repeat the main steps of the storyboard several times to get it "in the muscle."

Now, that is the main prototype. If you want to facilitate the movement to action further, you can add the six beliefs we worked with in the previous chapter—"It is important and worth it. It is possible. It is appropriate. I am capable. I am worthy and worth it. And I have the permission and support."

This should give the coachee the foundations of an effective storyboard. There will still be more details to work out and, of course, there will be the inevitable obstacles. But we think you'll find these steps of creating a compelling future very helpful and very useful.

To fill in more of the details related to the storyboard you have started, you can then go to Stage 2 of the process.

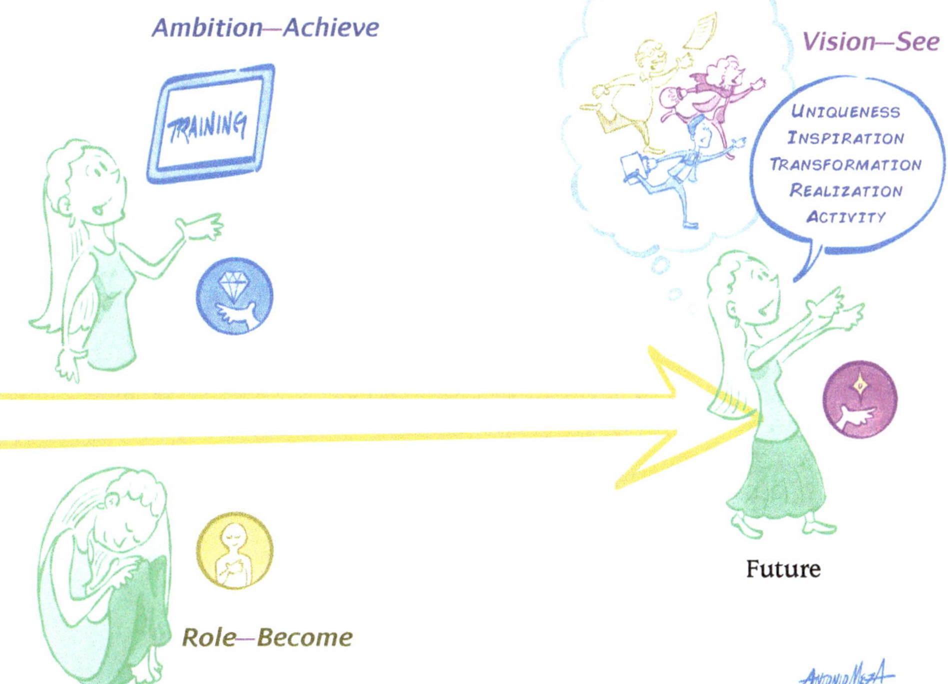

Stage 2: Aligning Levels of Change—Moving from Vision to Action

As we pointed out earlier, Stage 2 of the process is filling in the bottom part of the levels pyramid. As you start moving into action, you are going to need these other levels of resources. This is the idea of moving from vision into action. You connect your vision and your sense of identity to the values and beliefs that express and support them; and align those with the capabilities that are necessary to produce and guide the actions to take in a particular environmental context. This is a process we call **alignment**.

This process is especially useful in challenging situations as it activates multiple levels of resources.

The basic prototype involves exploring the following set of questions.

* *Where and when do you really need to be aligned? What external context or situation is challenging for you with respect to putting your intention into action?*

* *What do you want to do? If you were aligned with your intention, how would you act or respond in that situation?*

* *What capabilities do you need to be able to do that? What internal resources and knowhow are necessary to take the desired and appropriate actions?*

* *What beliefs and values support your capabilities and actions? Why is it important to enact your intention in that context?*

* *Who will you be or be more of if you are aligned with your intention? What would be your role and mission in that context?*

* *What is the bigger vision and purpose that you and your intention are in service of?*

One of the most effective ways to explore these questions is to physically take a series of steps that represent each level. We start by stepping into the environment where we want to really be aligned. Then, we take a step back from that and explore, "What do I want to do in that environment?" We then take another small step back and ask, "What inner resources do I need to effectively take those actions?" We take another small step back and identify, "What beliefs am I going to need?" With the next step we examine, "Who do I want to be? Who am I if I embody those beliefs, capabilities, and actions?" Finally, we step back and connect with the bigger vision to which we are aligning ourselves. Of course, we are also finding our somatic models for each of these levels.

We then step forward, moving from the vision back through each level to the environment, taking each step like a storyboard. We bring our vision together with our identity. Then connect our identity to the key values and beliefs; then the beliefs to the capabilities; the capabilities to the actions; and then bring those actions into the challenging environment we identified at the beginning of the process.

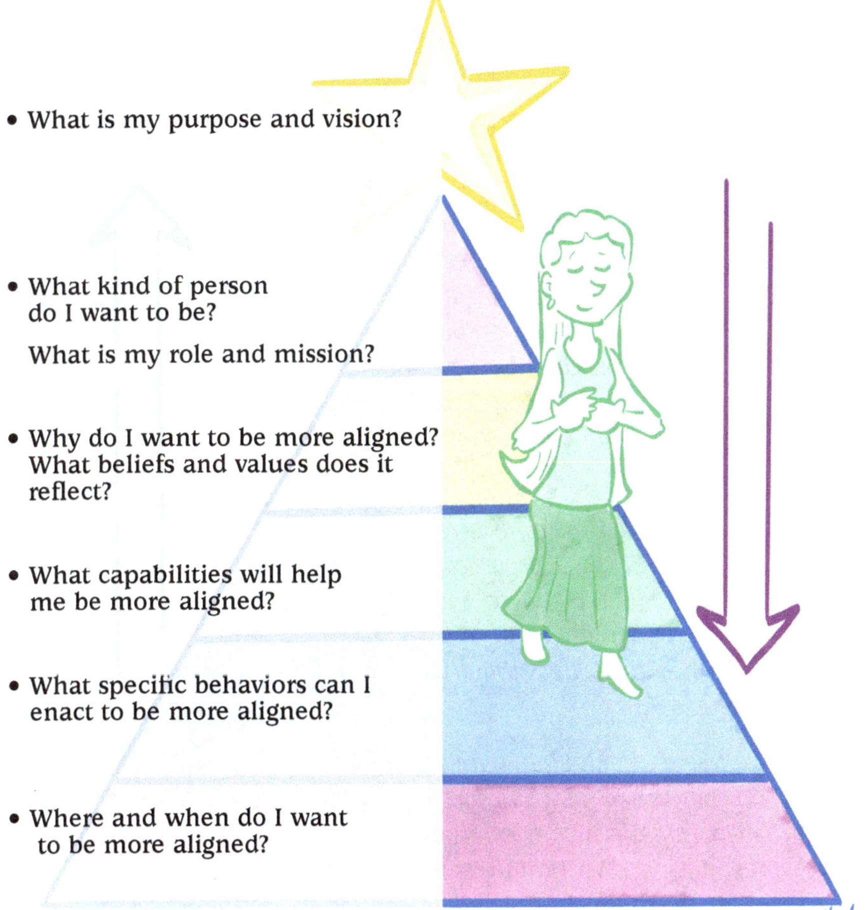

Alignment Demonstration

The following is a transcript of a demonstration of the Level Alignment Process that Robert did as part of a virtual training course.

Robert: *Hi George, we're going to be working with this process of getting aligned for action. If it's okay, it will be probably best to do it standing up if we can.*

George: *Okay.*

Robert: *Let's start with our COACH State before we go to what your intention is. Whatever is helpful for you to do some centering. To open the heart and open the mind. To bring some greater alertness and awareness. And connecting to your inner resources—to your intellect, to your compassion and passion, to your intuition. And coming into that state, where you can feel ready to do something important for you; ready to make a key step in your life. Is there anything that you want to share that helps you to really get into your COACH State and stay strongly in that COACH State?*

George: *Yes, I experience a stream going upwards from the Earth. I breathe the stream through my vertical axis up to the sky. And then, exhaling, I relax my head and shoulders and neck and heart and feel the stream going back down to the Earth.*

Robert: *Fantastic. When I join with you in that, I really feel that sense of strong groundedness and alignment. On a scale of zero to ten, where would you say your COACH State is right now?*

George: *Eight.*

Robert: *Eight, great. So, we're going to be working with this issue of alignment. So, what would be your intention? What is it that you really want to create more in your life?*

George: I want to feel myself more aligned in my intention of working with my clients in coaching and osteopathy and biodynamics.

Robert: Is there a particular context where this would be most important for you? Where and when would you like to feel that alignment?

George: That field is not part of my professional activity yet. And how I would understand that I have succeeded is that I would feel myself in that new environment and, while communicating with my clients, I would feel the same ease as I feel in my main professional activity, in my business that I've been doing for twenty years.

Robert: Great. That's really helpful. Let's try to put that intention into just a few words. Maybe something like, "I want to feel as much at ease in my new profession, as I do in the business, I've been doing for twenty years."

George: I want to feel in my new business activity that I'm standing strong on my foundation that gives me this feeling of calmness and certainty in talking to my new clients.

Robert: Yeah, that's great. If you were going to try to say that in just five words, what would be those words?

George: I want to speak confidently, feeling my foundation.

Robert: Great. So, speak confidently, feeling your foundation.

George: I speak confidently feeling my foundation. [Extends arms out in front of him with palms facing the ground and steadily lowers his hands and arms.]

Robert: Yeah. I start to really feel that intention strongly. And it looks like you're already starting to have a gesture for that.

George: *That's the gesture.* [Repeats the gesture.] *Be confident, feeling my foundation.*

Robert: [Mirrors the gesture.] *Great. What image comes to you with that?*

George: *I can see myself somewhere in the mountains standing on the rock in front of a big valley feeling this wind coming from this valley and having this sensation of flight, of flying.* [Opens arms wide like wings.] *And then there is sensation of opportunity and I can feel that the wind blowing to my face brings me this sensation of feeling my foundation.* [Extends arms out in front of him with palms facing the ground and steadily lowers his hands and arms.]

Robert: *So fantastic. That's actually a really lovely complement because you have this one out here* [opens arms wide like wings] *and then this* [extends arms out in front of him with palms facing the ground and steadily lowers his hands and arms.]. *Taking that image and those words and that gesture, let's really connect strongly to that intention. So, see the image, make the gestures and say the words. What happens?*

George: *I want to speak confidently feeling my foundation.* [Makes the two gestures.] *I get the sense of energetic flow, I get the sense of, it's flowing. And that sensation of energy, I can almost feel myself sweating.*

Robert: *Great. So, how strongly do you feel connected to that intention right now? Zero to ten.*

George: *I would say nine.*

Robert: *Yeah, looks like it. So, we have that sense of your center, your intention, and now when we go to our generative state, what resource from your field can help you and support you to achieve that intention?*

Environment

George: *For me, my resource is driving, driving a car.*

Robert: *Driving a car, okay. Say a little more.*

George: *It brings me pleasure. And even if I'm taking a really, really long journey, it's just the posture that bothers me. But other than that, I feel totally emerged and I immerse in this sensation of driving.*

Robert: *It's interesting because I also get this sense, that that brings out some playful energy for you.*

George: *Playful is joyful.*

Robert: *Yeah, great.*

George: *There's some kind of small competition but I can feel this lightness and cautiousness, like being cautious at the same time.*

Robert: *That's great. To me, there's a lot of generativity in that. So now, we're going to put all this together as we start moving into action. So, as you think concretely about that, what's a big step that you're going to need to take for your intention? To really bring this into reality, what's going to be one of the big challenges for you to do?*

George: *I have to create this practice for myself. Each and every day, I speak to two people that I've never known before, never met before, so they would feel immersed and interested in this discussion.*

Robert: *Great. So, as you daily begin to build your practice, you're going to be speaking with new people that you've never met before.*

George: *Yes, total strangers. I would just come up to them on the streets and talk to them. And I would be in COACH State while speaking to them, so nothing would be able to frighten me.*

Robert: *Okay. So, speaking to perfect strangers. So, here's what we're going to do. This is going to be our practice now. In a moment I'm going to ask you to take a step forward, like you're putting yourself into that situation. You're meeting and you're going to begin to speak to a perfect stranger. This is the bottom of the pyramid—the concrete* **where and when***. You can use either memory or imagination to put yourself into that concrete context. Okay?*

George: *Yes.* [Steps forward into the **environment** location.]

Robert: *Step, into it. And what you want to do is you're seeing that situation as you were there approaching this perfect stranger. And then you can take a little step back and explore the question, "What will you do, if you're speaking confidently from your foundation, what is it that you do? How are you speaking?*

George: [Takes a step back to the **behavior** location.] *When I started doing that, I felt myself kind of squeezing myself in, kind of crouching. But then I realized that I feel this energy coming from inside and it felt like I'm blossoming. And then I finally realized that being in this situation is not a problem for me anymore.* [Lengthens his spine and stands erect yet relaxed.] *And when I straighten up, I realized that it's not me speaking, it's the Earth speaking through me. And I felt like this energy, of course, is coming through me and my words are only just on the frames that are framing this energy that's not me. And I'm bringing this energy of Earth into existence.*

Robert: *That's beautiful. Wow, that gives me shivers. So, take a small step back from that and our next level is, "What capabilities come to you from this? What are you now capable to do?"*

Behavior

Capabilities

George: [Steps back to **capabilities** location.] *Now, I'm capable of speaking calmly, confidently speaking from the center of my belly. And no matter what I say, people would be really interested to hear that from me.*

Robert: *Great. Take another little step back and the next question is, "What are the beliefs that you have? What beliefs come to you when you are able to be aligned in that state?"*

George: [Steps back to **values and beliefs** location.] *When I align all my centers, I get this belief about what I would say. And that's not really comfortable because I can feel it kind of messes me up. It interferes with me.*

Robert: *So, let's find what the belief is that you need here.*

George: *What I thought is that what I need is to start speaking with this playfulness and kind of stretching my voice. And then I would get from the field the ideas and the meaning of what I'd be able to say.*

Robert: *So, let's put that into a belief. What would you need to believe in order for that to happen?*

George: *I would need to believe that I could trust in my intuition.*

Robert: *So, the belief is, "I can trust my intuition?"*

George: *Yes, I do have this belief and I can say that I really trust my intuition.*

Robert: *What is your somatic model for trusting your intuition?*

George: *I trust my intuition.* [Brings both hands to his diaphragm, raises his head and lengthens his spine.] *I trust my intuition.* [Repeats the gesture.] *I trust my intuition.* [Repeats the gesture.] *I can feel it's strengthening, and it also strengthens my body.*

Robert: *Fantastic. Take another little step back. Now, if you align these things in that situation and you have that behavior of straightening up and standing tall; and the capability to speak calmly and confidently, channeling the energy from the Earth; and this belief that you can trust your intuition; what is your identity? Who do you become?*

George: [Steps back to the **identity** location.] *At first, what comes to my mind is confident and calm, and strong.*

Robert: *What would be your symbol for this identity, this confident, calm, strong identity?*

George: *I get this image of an oak tree. I see this strong tree confidently standing there being both agile and strong.*

Robert: *Fantastic. Take another little step back. The final question for this alignment is, "When you can be in that identity of the oak tree and believe that you can trust your intuition, and have this capability to speak from the Earth as you straighten up and stand tall, what is your purpose? What is that bigger purpose that you are contributing to or serving?"*

Beliefs

Identity

George: [Steps back to the **purpose** location.] *It is the harmony of strength and sensitivity.* [Folds his hands over his diaphragm, opens and extends them out in front of him, then brings them back to his diaphragm.] *It's all about strength and sensitivity and also being careful and taking care of the people that I'll be talking to.*

Robert: *Yes.* [Mirrors the gesture.] *And you're already making your somatic model of that. What is the image that you have of this purpose?*

George: [Repeats the gesture.] *It's when I touch the leaf of a tree. And I can hear how it springs back when I touch it.*

Robert: *Yes. Wonderful. So, the last thing we're going to do is to take that purpose and that image of that touching the tree and springing back. And we step forward and connect that to your identity of the oak tree.* [George and Robert step forward to the **identity** location and make the somatic model associated with that.] *And then to the belief that I can trust my intuition.* [George and Robert step forward to the **values and beliefs** location and make the somatic model associated with that.] *And to this capability to speak from the Earth.* [George and Robert step forward to the **capabilities** location and make the somatic model associated with that.] *And to the action of straightening up and standing tall.* [George and Robert step forward to the **behavior** location and make the somatic model associated with that.] *So that when you speak to the stranger, it's like touching the leaf, you're the oak tree, you're trusting, and you're letting that wisdom of the Earth come through you as you stand tall. So that each word is an expression of all of these levels of alignment.*

George: *I get this image of several leaves and really warm summer wind that is shimmering these leaves.*

Robert: *And let's take all of that and really bring it into that concrete situation. With all those resources, you step into that situation. You are on the street and there's the stranger. And you begin to speak. How does that feel?*

George: [Steps forward into the **environment** location.] *I can feel this flow. There is still some nervousness but it's more like a distant sound. In fact, this feeling of being nervous kind of highlights the sensitivity; it allows me to bring this sense of care into the conversation.*

Robert: *Yeah, that's important. It sounds like it's an important team member.*

George: *Yes, yes. Exactly that.*

Robert: *So, do you feel ready to go for it?*

George: *Yes. Absolutely!* [Smiles broadly.]

Robert: *Fantastic.*

George: *Thank you so much for you work and being so caring. I was looking at your picture and the image was really small in my screen. But just looking at your movements, I could feel this mist, not just a mist, and maybe the state of lightness.*

Robert: *Yes. And I could certainly feel a strong sense of connection with you too. Is there anything else that you would want to share about what was most effective or useful from the session?*

George: *The most important thing for me was how the strength transformed itself into something more resembling sensitivity and caring. That was something that was most useful for me. When I was saying these words, I saw a picture of an elephant. And the elephant is really big, but at the same time, it can be really gentle and flexible.*

Robert: *Yeah. And they have a very sensitive trunk.*

George: *Yeah. That's exactly how I felt.*

Robert: *Fantastic. I send you my full support for your journey ahead.*

George: *Thank you.*

STRONG, GENTLE AND FLEXIBLE ELEPHANT.

THE HARMONY OF STRENGTH AND SENSITIVITY.
I CAN TRUST MY INTUITION.
I AM AN OAK TREE.
HELLO!
SPEAK CONFIDENTLY.
SPEAK TO TWO PEOPLE I HAVE NEVER MET BEFORE.
EVERYDAY IN THE CITY.
Antonio Meza

Alignment Demonstration

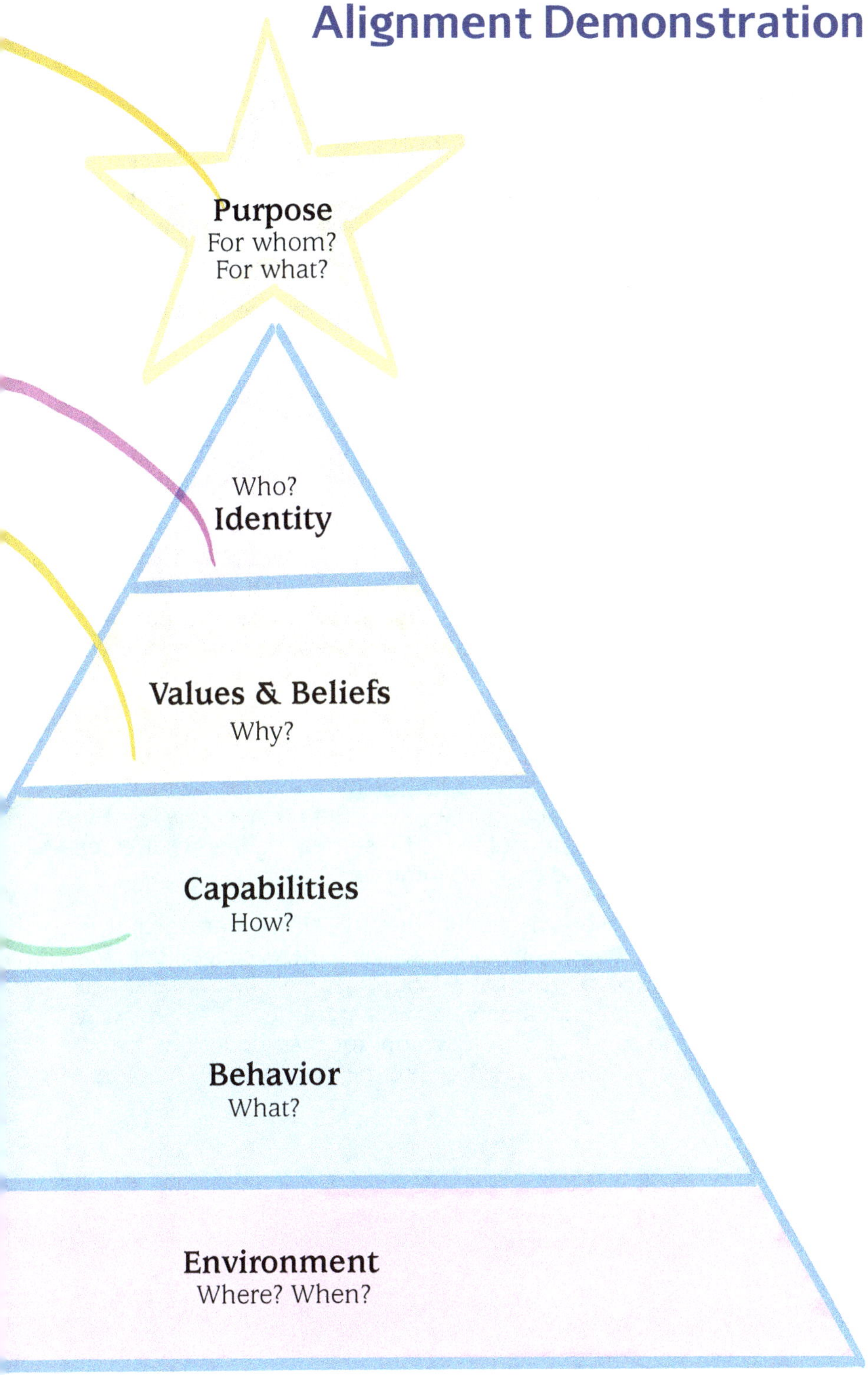

Summary

The Alignment process is a way of enriching **Step 4** where we are bringing in these different levels of resources to support moving into action. The focus is on enacting an intention in an important or challenging external context that requires multiple levels of resources in order to be successful. In George's case, this was walking up to a complete stranger on the street and engaging them in a conversation about his new professional interest. So, that's the first question, "What's the external situation where you are meeting a challenge in putting your intention into action?"

Then, we explore the second question, which is, "If you are aligned with your intention, what would you do? How will you stand? How will you speak? How will you act if you are aligned in this situation?" In George's case, a key behavior was straightening his posture and standing tall.

Then we go to the next level, which has to do with the capabilities necessary to take those actions. If you are aligned with your intention, what are the capabilities you will need access to? What are the capabilities that are available? In the demonstration with George, he talked about "speaking calmly and confidently" and speaking from the center of his belly as if the Earth was speaking through him.

And then we go to the level of beliefs. "What is the belief that you have if you are aligned? And what belief helps you to be aligned?" Of course, this could involve any of the key beliefs that we have been presenting in this volume. It could also be something like what came up for George; that he could trust his intuition.

Then the next question is about identity. "If you are acting in alignment with your intention and you have these capabilities and these beliefs in that context, who are you?" George's first answer was "a strong, confident, grounded person." It is at this level that we really often like to add in some kind of a symbol for that identity as a kind of an anchor. And that's where George got the symbol of an oak tree.

And the final question is, "What is the bigger purpose?" We often make the point that courage comes from being connected to something bigger than yourself; something beyond your ego. So, this is where you're getting a sense of this bigger connection. What is it that you are serving? And that's where George had that beautiful image of touching the leaves of the tree. And he was saying that's where his sense of strength turned into sensitivity; and that was very important and powerful for him.

Once we have all of these levels clarified, we want to move back down the levels, from purpose to environment, to make sure that they are all aligned and connected together. One of the most powerful ways to do that is through the somatic models. In the demonstration, George was already very engaged somatically so it was not generally necessary to ask him for a somatic model, because he was already showing them. When doing this process with clients it will be important to ensure that they have somatic models for each level, because you don't want it just to be an intellectual, verbal conversation. You're really trying to fully engage these different levels of resources.

The process is completed by connecting purpose to identity to belief to capabilities and the actions, so that, when you step into the reality of that situation, it's not just about the behavior. All of those levels are there. In George's case, it is not just that he is talking to a stranger, he is actually fulfilling a purpose. He is bringing this deeper identity symbolized by the oak tree into action through these key beliefs and capabilities.

So, the main idea at **Step 4** is that you are beginning to do a kind of a virtual dress rehearsal. And the more of these different levels you get activated and involved, the more it feels real and doable. Because these are going to be the resources that you are going to need in order to truly bring something into action and make it real.

It also helps to prepare you for transforming the inevitable obstacles that will emerge as we go to **Step 5**.

Courage

It is in the small things we see it.
The child's first step,
as awesome as an earthquake.
The first time you rode a bike,
wallowing up the sidewalk.
The first spanking when your heart
went on a journey all alone.
When they called you crybaby
or poor or fatty or crazy
and made you into an alien,
you drank their acid
and concealed it.

Later,
if you have endured great despair,
then you did it alone,
getting a transfusion from the fire,
picking the scabs off your heart,
then wringing it out like a sock.
Next, my kinsman, you powdered your sorrow,
you gave it a back rub
and then you covered it with a blanket
and after it had slept a while
it woke to the wings of the roses
and was transformed.

Later,
when you face old age and its natural conclusion
your courage will still be shown in the little ways.
each spring will be a sword you'll sharpen,
those you love will live in a fever of love,
and you'll bargain with the calendar
and at the last moment
when death opens the back door
you'll put on your carpet slippers
and stride out.

—Anne Sexton

Chapter 6

Step 5
Transforming Obstacles Into Resources

As we think about this idea of transforming obstacles, about changing problems into resources, we realize that we tend to meet certain common types of obstacles. And what we are calling an obstacle is anything that can come and create some form of CRASH. This involves some form of contraction, of reactivity, of analysis paralysis, of separation or disconnection from any of our three positive connections, and some form of hostility, or negative response.

Typical obstacles that come up in coaching are obviously emotional responses. But sometimes, it is also a critical voice. Frequently it will involve some type of negative repetitive behavioral habit or pattern, or a dysfunctional relationship. Other times obstacles take the form of institutional barriers or other limitations coming from the field that we are in. And of course, some will emerge from *limiting beliefs*.

Some of these obstacles are within us. Others are more in the field around us; and the internal and external obstacles often interact. Step 5 involves applying the skills and resources needed to help to transform these obstacles.

Three Brains in One

One important thing to realize is that, if we think about the notions of COACH State and CRASH State, neuroscientists will tell us that, instead of one brain, you actually have three brains. There is the reptilian brain; the mammal brain or the limbic brain; and then our "higher" centers—the cortex of the brain, the gray matter. When we are in a generative state, all of these are active; especially, the higher cortex.

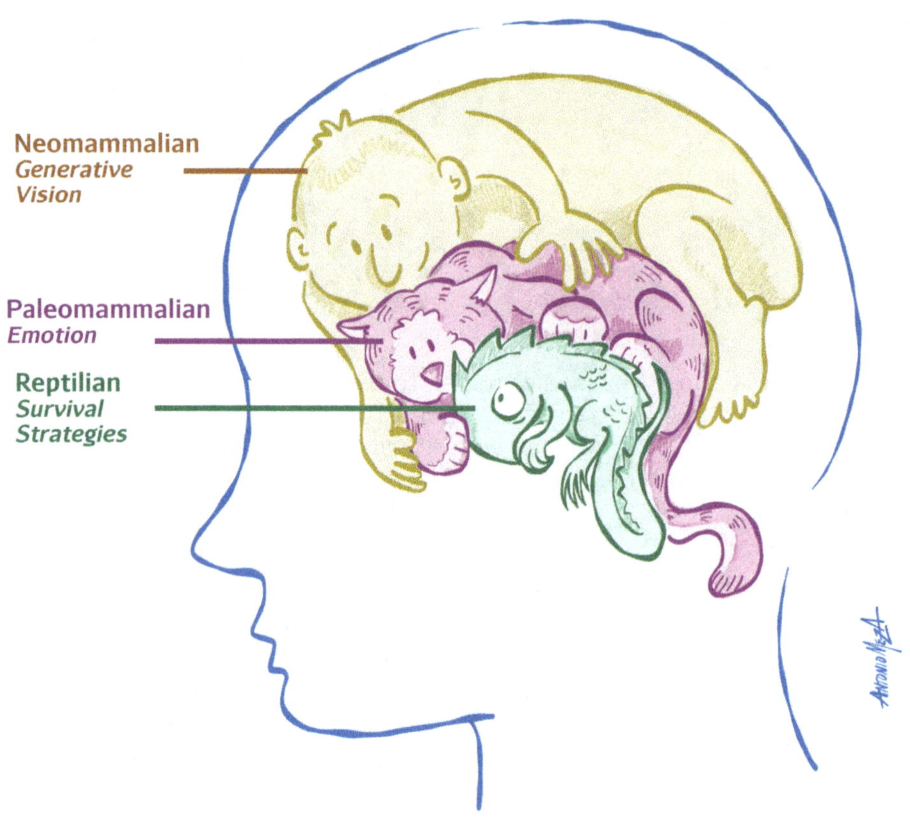

In a generative state the higher levels of our brain are "online."

The limbic brain, this mammal brain, doesn't have language. It doesn't have the capacity for generative vision. It is more emotional. It's essentially the brain of a dog, or a cat, or a horse. If you think of interacting with a dog or a cat, that is similar to how this mammal part of us functions. As humans, we have the same reactions that every other mammal does. The dog sees a stranger, or sees another dog, and it barks. And we will have those types of reactions in ourselves.

In this regard, we sometimes will say to our clients that there is the bad news and the good news. The bad news is that no matter how much generative coaching you do, no matter how many drugs you take, no matter what your religion is, no matter how much you practice, you are going to have a mammal brain the rest of your life. Meaning, you are going to feel anger, fear, sadness, frustration, etc. They are never going to go away.

But the good news is that it does not have to be a problem. Because, when you can stay in a COACH State and a generative state, then those reactions can become resources. We have seen this in several of the demonstrations thus far in this book. George said at the end of the demonstration in the previous chapter, *"Well, I still feel nervous, but actually, that's not a problem. It's helping me to bring sensitivity and care into the conversation. The nervousness is an important part of the team."* In the demonstration with Alice, she said, *"I have this fear that I'm not fully ready."* But that feeling also became an important team member, reminding her to *"be more systematic and have a daily action plan."*

There are always going to be responses that come up from those lower brain centers. The problem with CRASH is that it starts to take the whole top part of the brain offline. So, then when I have the emotional reaction, it is only the emotional reaction. There is no generative creative transformation.

When you get really CRASHed, you get basically just into the reptilian brain. Reptiles don't even really feel emotion. They don't get angry. Think of a snake. A snake is not going to get angry at you and chase you. But a dog will. The snake is just totally reactive if it perceives a threat. So, it's just those survival reactions—attack, run away, freeze. When we go into these unconscious patterns, we are more or less just like a reptile.

So, we need to realize that these fundamental reactions and patterns will always be inside of us. But when we can stay centered and connected to our human presence—this higher cortical brain center—then instead of acting like a reptile or acting like a mammal, we actually start to take those same responses and feelings and become creative. Again, this is where we emphasize developing a positive skillful human relationship with whatever "negative" feeling or thought is coming through us.

The Inner Game

To help with that, we want to introduce the notion of the "inner game," which we think provides a helpful framework, especially for those of you who work in companies and businesses. People often ask us, "How do I explain generative coaching to people in a business that don't know anything about personal development?" One effective approach is to use this frame of the so-called inner game.

The notion of the inner game was developed by Timothy Gallwey. His first book was *The Inner Game of Tennis*. He has since written other books, such as *The Inner Game of Business*. Gallwey was a very high-level tennis player and was the captain of the Harvard University tennis team in the early 1960s. As a tennis pro, he was a very committed and competitive athlete. Of course, he was always trying to improve his performance; always trying to get better, trying to be his best. But he found that he encountered certain barriers such that, no matter how much he practiced physically, he wasn't significantly improving.

Then, in the early 1970s, he happened to take a class on meditation. To his surprise, he suddenly found that his tennis performance dramatically increased even though he wasn't doing any more physical practice. This led him to this realization about the relationship between the so-called outer game and the inner game. We have found this a really useful and important distinction to make in our coaching work.

According to Gallwey:

In every human endeavor there are two arenas of engagement: the outer and the inner. The outer game is played on an external arena to overcome external obstacles to reach an external goal. The inner game takes place within the mind of the player and is played against such obstacles as fear, self-doubt, lapses in focus, and limiting concepts or assumptions. The inner game is played to overcome the self-imposed obstacles that prevent an individual or team from accessing their full potential.

As this quote points out, in the outer game we have outer goals, outer resources and there are also outer obstacles. In the demonstration with George in the previous chapter, his outer game was to be able to go and speak to strangers about his new professional interests. He wanted to engage them and get them interested in what he was doing. That is the outer game; but that outer game is completely dependent on his inner game. And that inner game was to be confident and to be connected to his foundation. If we fail at our inner game, we are most likely going to fail at the outer game.

In fact, if I meet an outer obstacle with an inner obstacle, I have essentially an unsolvable problem. If I meet the same outer obstacle with my inner resources, I have a potentially achievable challenge. If my inner obstacle meets outer resources, it's my lucky day. And when inner resources meet outer resources, it's magic.

So, in the inner game, we have inner goals and inner resources and, of course, inner obstacles. As Timothy Gallwey points out, those inner obstacles are things like fear, loss of energy, and self-limiting beliefs and ideas. On the other hand, when we succeed in our inner game, we are in this state of "flow" or "zone of excellence." This is clearly very similar to what we call our COACH state and our generative state. There is a sense of self-confidence that you could call a "humble authority;" which is confidence without arrogance. We're humble but we are certain and self-confident. We are relaxed, but we are also ready in the body. And our mind is focused yet also spacious.

So, we have this very interesting combination of complements that we have seen this in a number of the demonstrations. George, for example, was talking about being confident and also cautious. He also described being strong but also sensitive. So, in this zone, in the COACH State, we can hold these complements in a creative way. Because, very often, if somebody is relaxed, they're not ready. If they are ready, they are not relaxed. It's the same with the mind. If people are focused, they are not spacious. Or if they are spacious, there's no focus. But when we can hold them both in balance, we enter this flow state and experience a type of effortless excellence.

The opposite of being in this inner zone of excellence and the state of flow, is what we call CRASH. And one of the things that I really like to point out, especially to people in businesses, is that limitations in people limit their performance, which in turn limits the organization. And it is especially true that limitations within the leaders are going to limit the whole organization.

Inner Game Skills

So, there are a number of key inner game skills; all of which we have already been engaging in this and the previous volumes of *Generative Coaching*. The first is greater *self-awareness*—more awareness of my thoughts, my body, my feelings, and what's happening inside. A second is what we call *self-modeling*. That is, I pay attention to what is working and what doesn't work and explore the question, *"What is the difference that makes the difference?" What makes the difference between COACH and CRASH? When I'm in my COACH State, how do I know it?* This is what we were doing in the "Finding your Center" process in Chapter 2. Self-modeling also involves finding examples of when I have been in my COACH State and exploring, "What is common to those examples?"

The inner game skill of *self-calibration* (or self-scaling) comes as a result of self-modeling. Once we have tracked the differences that make a difference, we can ask, "On a scale of zero to ten, what level am I at right now?" Once I know what a strong COACH State is like, I can now say, "Okay, where am I with respect to that?" If zero is complete CRASH and ten is being in my peak COACH State, what level is my current state?

Self-adjustment involves taking steps to increase the level of a particular state. What can be done to shift it to a more optimum level? What can I influence with respect to my inner experience or physiology that would increase my COACH State from, say, six to seven or eight? And, once we successfully make an adjustment, we want to apply *self-anchoring* in order to stabilize and sustain that level of the state. This involves things like finding somatic models, symbols or external objects that help us to remember and reinforce these resourceful states.

Self-Awareness　　　　Self-Modeling　　　　Self-Calibration

In summary, the **inner game skills** are:

1. **Self-Awareness**—Increasing your awareness of the cognitive and somatic elements making up and influencing your inner state and mindset. *What are you aware of? (Images, sounds, feelings, sensations, etc.)*

2. **Self-Modeling**—Determining which cognitive and somatic elements are associated with optimal performance (generative COACH States) and which ones produce "neuromuscular lock" (degenerative CRASH States). *What are the "differences that make a difference" in terms of optimal mindset/performance?*

3. **Self-Calibration**—Assessing the current state of those key elements with respect to their optimum values. *How fully are you in your optimal state in comparison to your peak? (zero to ten)*

4. **Self-Adjustment**—Adjusting the key elements to produce a more appropriate or optimum expression and exploring the new options that creates. *What can you do to shift to a more optimum level?*

5. **Self-Anchoring**—Finding cues and triggers that will help you to remember and solidify an optimum expression of your mindset and inner state. *What will help you to remember/hold this level?*

Self-Adjustment

Self-Anchoring

There is a very interesting quote related to these inner skills game attributed to the Chinese philosopher Lao Tzu.

Watch your thoughts,
they become words.

Watch your words,
they become actions.

Watch your actions,
they become habits.

Watch your habits,
they become your character.

Watch your character,
it becomes your destiny.

The quote offers an interesting insight into how our inner game relates to the Levels of Change pyramid. Repeated behaviors become capabilities; capabilities reinforce beliefs; beliefs fashion the expression of identity; and our identity shapes our purpose or destiny. The key implication of this quotation is that directing or changing our destiny begins with our thoughts—our inner game. As we say in Generative Change work: "Your reality is a function of your state!"

Applying Emotional Intelligence

Another key part of our inner game, especially when it comes to transforming obstacles, has to do with emotional intelligence. When we apply emotional intelligence, there are several different steps and stages. If you think about what we have been doing when we meet some kind of seemingly negative emotional obstacle, such as fear, frustration, anger, etc., the first thing we need to do is to recognize it. Be aware that it is there. The second thing is to acknowledge it, without judgment. That is why we say: "That's interesting."

Next, we create that space for it. We are holding it from this larger place of what the Buddhists would call "equanimity." That is our COACH State from which we can say: "Welcome."

Then, we seek to understand it. What is its positive intention? What is it doing there? "I'm sure it makes sense. Something is needing to be heard, or held, or healed."

Finally we resource it. We bring resources through our generative state to it and that is what helps to make the transformation. Once it's transformed, it can become integrated. Instead of being an obstacle, it becomes a valued team member.

This is the path that we have followed over and over again whenever we meet obstacles.

1. *Recognizing (calibrating)* the presence of a particular emotional state

2. *Acknowledging* the presence of the state without judgment

3. Holding the emotional state in an environment of "equanimity" (*making space* for it)

4. *Understanding* the emotional state and its function (positive intention)

5. *Resourcing* the emotional state by connecting it to other complementary emotions and states

6. *Transforming* or refining the expression of the emotional state to be more harmonious and productive with respect to its positive intention

7. *Integrating* the emotional state as a contributing part of a larger system

The Example of the "Miracle on the Hudson"

A powerful example of this, and one we often use when presenting principles of generative change to business managers and leaders, is the so-called "Miracle on the Hudson." In February of 2009, a passenger jet was taking off out of New York City when suddenly, right at the critical point of takeoff, it unexpectedly encountered a large flock of geese. And so many birds were pulled into the engines of the airplane that both engines shut down simultaneously. This becomes a very interesting moment for the pilot of the jet. Because if he CRASHes in his inner game, we can be pretty certain that the airplane is going to crash in the outer game. If he freezes or if he goes into analysis paralysis, two hundred people die.

In addition, he has to be generative. He has to do something he has never done before—that nobody has ever done before—in order to safely land that plane. There is nothing in the pilot manual that says: "Okay, if you are at a thousand meters over New York City and both engines are gone, here's what to do." The pilot has to go into a generative state and do something nobody has done before. He has never flown a plane with no engines or landed it. With no engines, he can't turn around and go back to the airport. He has to very quickly and creatively find a way to land this plane in a city. He had something like less than three minutes from the time that the engines went out until the plane was going to be on the ground.

The very interesting thing you must realize is that, paradoxically, in that kind of a very dangerous situation, the first thing you have to do is relax. Because if you're in a CRASH State, it's going to be a disaster. And in fact, this pilot (Chesley Sullenberger) was able to stay in a COACH State and quickly wonder: "Where do I land the plane?" He could see he was close enough to the Hudson River that he could bring the plane and land it on the river without landing on any boats. But he also had to maneuver close enough to boats that could come and get the people off the airplane before it sank.

And the miracle was his being able to bring that plane down with no engines, land it on the river, without the plane breaking up, because it's very difficult to land an airplane on water. And everybody on the plane was able to get off and they all survived. In fact, the pilot himself walked the whole length of the airplane at least three times to make sure nobody else was still was in the aircraft before he got off. There weren't even any really serious injuries. In fact, the only people that got injured were the ones who panicked and injured themselves after the plane had stopped.

Now, the interesting thing was, when the pilot was interviewed afterward, the reporters said, "Wow, you seemed so calm during this whole thing, and you made this miracle. Weren't you at all afraid?" The pilot's answer was very interesting because he said, *Are you crazy? I've never been more afraid in my life."* However, he then added, *"I've also never been more calm in my life."* So, they asked him: "How could you be more calm in your life when you've never been more afraid in your life? How was that possible? How did you stay so calm?" And he gave several answers which are very interesting from the generative change perspective.

His first one was, "*practice*." Obviously, he had—thankfully—never had to practice that particular outer game sequence before. But he had had a lot of practice with his inner game. He said: *"As a professional, it's my responsibility to stay in the best version of myself, no matter what is going on outside."* In fact, he used the metaphor of practicing his inner game being like making "*deposits*" into his "*bank of experience*." He commented that this allowed him to *"make a big withdrawal that day."* This is why we say that practice is important. Because there's no way he could have anticipated that "maybe when I'm taking off, I'm going to run into birds today." You don't know. And he has no time to think: "Oh, what's six-step technique should I use?" It has to already be there. We say practice is what brings something into the muscle.

Making a big withdrawal out of the bank of experience.

A second thing he said, which was interesting, given what we were exploring in the previous chapter, was: *"I was afraid for myself, for my own ego, but I was the pilot. I am the captain of the plane and my role, and my mission is to keep everybody safe. So, I was afraid for me, but I was calm for those two hundred people."* And this is the power of having a **role** and a **mission** and keeping connection with your mission. It's that mission, and that role, that identity, that's going to give you the courage and the determination to do miracles.

The third thing he said was: *"It also really helped that the crew stayed so calm and the passengers stayed calm."* So, they asked the crew: "Well, why did you stay so calm?" And their answer was, *"Well, because the pilot was calm and the passengers stayed calm."* They said to the passengers: "Why were you calm?" The passengers all said: *"Well, the captain sure seemed calm and the crew was calm."* So, here you can see how one person can create a powerful and resourceful *field*.

By the way, the final thing that the captain shared, which sounds paradoxical, was about the importance of his father's suicide. Some years before this event his father had committed suicide. And you might think, "Well, that doesn't sound like a resource. That sounds like a trauma." And it was. In fact, this pilot said: "That was the most traumatic thing in my life." But instead of going into some big state of CRASH, he *transformed* all that grief into the commitment and determination to never just be a *"bystander"*; that if he could do anything to help somebody, he would do it. He said: *"My father's suicide was very present for me in those moments when I was landing the plane. And one of the reasons I was so committed to save all of those people was because I hadn't been able to save my father."*

It is interesting to see so many of our generative change principles operating in this illustration of how you create an outer miracle. Clearly, it starts with the inner game. And it starts with practice.

An Inner Game Practice—Slow Down, Pause, Breathe, Center

Often, at the beginning of a Generative Coaching session with a client, we might say: "We know we're going to be meeting potential obstacles in the session and in this work. And when we do, there are just four things we want to remember. The first is to slow down. Because when you slow down, you stay aware. Secondly, we pause. Pausing allows us to connect and reconnect more deeply with our inner resources. Third, we breathe. Breathing allows us to open more space to be present with what is happening. And fourth, we center. We gather ourselves and come back to our inner source." This is a way of practicing resilience. It's how to quickly get back to our inner zone of excellence.

This simple practice becomes important to initiate as soon as you meet an obstacle. Rather than speeding up or trying to do something, we slow down. We pause. We breathe. And we center. Very interestingly, if you think of the pilot who only has three minutes to land the plane with no engines, obviously, he has to react quickly. But if you've ever had one of these types of experiences or if you talk to people that have had these emergencies, they say time suddenly slows way down. As we slow down our inner dialogue and other conscious cognitive functions, we become more aware of everything else and there is more time for our creative unconscious to respond appropriately.

To somatically support this practice, we will often incorporate the following non-verbal signals.

We will practice making these signals together with the client so that they become like automatic anchors. Then we can use these signals any time during the coaching session as a reminder. And we encourage the client can also use them as well.

This practice can be particularly powerful when we combine the verbal "*mantras*" connected with the stages of emotional intelligence with these somatic signals.

1. Slow Down—*That's interesting.*

2. Pause—*I am sure it makes sense.*

3. Breathe—*Something is needing to be heard, or held, or healed.*

4. Center—*Welcome.*

Developing a "Second Skin"

Another useful resource and inner game practice for transforming obstacles is developing a *"second skin."* This is something that can be important for our clients, but it is also really important for us as coaches. Because, again, we have these mirror neurons, and we can get into fields that can be very disturbed. One of the main reasons that people CRASH and contract and separate is because they are trying to protect themselves. In a toxic field, it is natural to try to put up barriers or to try to disassociate. Paradoxically this way of trying to be safe ends up making us less present and generative and ultimately even more at risk.

The notion of a skin is very interesting. On the one hand, your skin protects you and separates you from others. It is selective but, on the other hand, it is also receptive. We connect through the skin as well. A second skin is a kind of energetic skin. It is a type of energetic insulation that protects us from potential disturbances coming from the various fields around us without disconnecting us from the important knowledge and information contained in those fields. It keeps us safe but at the same time, present and connected.

Skin is a type of membrane that has pores which filter the flow of energy, material and information that pass between what is outside of the membrane and what is held within it. A second skin determines, on the one hand, how much of our own energy is contained on the inside and how much is released into the world. On the other hand, it connects us to the outside world through touch, but also regulates the impact of outer energies and influences by filtering what aspects of them are allowed to enter.

There are many fields around us. We have temperature fields, and there are also electromagnetic fields that come out of our body. So, just like that pilot, when he is able to stay calm, he begins to create this field of calmness for others. And this is the same thing we do with our clients. We are often influencing them through our field.

Practice—Developing and Applying a Second Skin

The following is a practice you can use to create a second skin for yourself and to also help your clients to create a second skin for themselves.

We begin by coming into a good COACH State. Take time to just slow down, pause, breathe, and center. Enter into a state of relaxed readiness in the body, and focused spaciousness in the mind. Connect to the feeling of humble authority; of self-confidence without arrogance.

And then when you can really be in that state, take your two hands and hold them in front of you with the palms facing each other. And become very, very sensitive to the space between your palms. For this process, we use both our actual sensation and our imagination. As neuroscience has demonstrated, imagination is just as important in our brain as ongoing sensation and perception, and memory.

What you want to do is to feel the field created by this resourceful COACH State, this state of flow, between your hands. And notice its qualities. For example, physically, does it have a temperature or texture? Also use your imagination. If you could see it, would it have a color? Does it have a brightness? Is it moving or still? Perhaps it might even have a tone or a sound. Just explore, using sensation and imagination, the qualities of this field generated by your COACH State.

Second Skin

When you can sense that field between the hands, then turn your palms towards your body so you can also feel that resourceful field between your hands and your body. That is going to be your second skin. And this second skin is not like a bubble or a spacesuit. It is actually the presence of a larger self. Instead of feeling disconnected, you are actually feeling bigger. You occupy a bigger space.

Then, with your hands, sculpt this second skin around your whole body; this larger self. As you sculpt with your hands, visualize the presence of the skin having the qualities you saw between your hands. If it has a sound, that can surround you as well. Imagine that you are feeling and sensing presence of a bigger you. Experience both the sense of security but also a bigger sense of connection, as if you have a larger personal space.

Walking through the airport with my second skin.

For me, I always feel this is the presence of my potential. And when I remember my second skin and I'm in that second skin, then people can be in really big CRASH States around me and I can actually be very compassionate. But at the same time, I'm not getting drawn into or overwhelmed by what's happening. For example, if I am walking through an airport, I walk in my second skin. When I'm with a client, I am listening, especially if they are meeting an obstacle, from within that second skin.

To explore the value and effectiveness of your second skin, you can think of a challenging outer game situation, where it is difficult for you to stay in your COACH State because you feel a disruptive influence in the field related to that situation. For example, some people struggle when they are in a gathering of their family members of origin and find themselves back in old family patterns. Or perhaps there are certain clients where you find yourself feeling caught up in their drama or drained and exhausted at the end of a session.

Use your second skin...even in family reunions!

Pick a situation where you find it difficult to easily remain in your COACH State. Feeling and visualizing the second skin in this larger self around you, take a step and put yourself into that situation as fully as you can. Sometimes, to remind myself of that second skin, I briefly face my palms toward one another and sense the field that is there. It is the same outer game but now you have something new for your inner game. And just notice what difference that makes in your inner game. When you can stay more calm, centered and confident in your inner game, what new becomes possible in that outer situation?

Like any practice, it is useful to do this multiple times and with different situations. Like the pilot in the Miracle on the Hudson, it becomes another "*deposit*" in your bank of experience that you can draw upon.

The following is an outline of another basic prototype for practicing strengthening and using your second skin.

1. Identify a context in which you became overwhelmed, lost in or assaulted by a disturbed or "shadow" field.

2. Step into that situation. How and where do you experience the impact of this disturbed energy?

3. Step out and re-enter COACH State.

4. Hold the palms of your hands facing one another so that they are almost touching. Use sensation and imagination to feel the COACH field between them.

5. Move your hands and arms to move into a position as if you were about to embrace someone. Feel the presence of the field within your embrace.

6. Bring this field around the you who has been caught in the difficult situation. Imagine that you are sculpting and creating a "*second skin*" around that you.

7. Step into the you who is now surrounded by this second skin and use your hands to be sure that you can feel the presence of the energetic skin around you.

Holding Difficult Feelings

Thus far in this chapter, we have presented the notion of the inner game and the importance of engaging emotional intelligence. As we have established, emotional intelligence is about recognizing that some emotion is there and acknowledging its presence without judgment. That's this idea of, *"That's interesting."* Then we create an inner holding environment for it where we can be with it without becoming it. This is this idea of welcoming it. From there, we can seek to better understand it: *"I'm sure it makes sense. There's some positive intention. Something is needing to be held, heard and/or healed."* Once we can understand that positive intention, we can bring in other resources. In terms of the image presented earlier of the three different brains, we can connect this mammal brain to the human brain. This is this idea of: *"Accessing resources that allow us to include this emotion into a bigger holon."* That automatically will bring a transformation. And once the expression of the emotion is transformed, it can be integrated in a positive way as an important *"team member."*

Hopefully, you'll recognize this as the main set of steps that we are always taking in generative coaching when we meet obstacles, especially emotional obstacles. Often though, when we first meet these emotions, either in ourselves or when our clients are meeting them, it is natural to experience some amount of initial CRASH. This is where having some of the practices and habits we presented in the previous section become really helpful.

Remembering to "slow down, pause, breathe and center," and just being able to do that very simply and quickly is already going to start to make a big difference. Adding those verbal mantras can make it even more effective: *"That's interesting. I'm sure it makes sense. Something is really wanting to be honored, heard, held, perhaps healed. Welcome."* Once we can welcome the feeling, we have another resource, which is our second skin that helps us to connect to our larger self. Then we can begin to explore the positive intention behind the emotion and what resources we might bring to it.

We are going to put all this together in a practice called "Holding Difficult Feelings." In the course of our lives, we are constantly facing disruptions and challenges and are probably going to be encountering many difficult feelings every day. There are going to be moments that we feel frustrated, afraid, irritated, etc. Instead of either fighting them, suppressing them, avoiding them, or letting them take us over, we have this other choice—to have an emotionally intelligent relationship with them.

A key part of this process is a very interesting and important question that comes from the work of Virginia Satir. Virginia was a family therapist and one of the people modeled during the original creation of NLP. When she was working with a family, there would inevitably be a point when the members of the family would trigger one another and create some type of CRASH that would often be expressed as blame or defensiveness directed at another family member or members.

Virginia would intervene by having people come back to their own inner game. She would take the attention off the other person. Instead of saying, "What are they doing?" she would say: "So, how do you feel?" Remember how one of those big regrets in Chapter 3 was: "I didn't actually express how I felt." So, the family member might respond by saying, "I feel frustrated," or, "I feel really angry." Virginia would then ask this very interesting follow up question. She would say, "And how do you feel about feeling that way?"

In a CRASH State, people are rarely even aware of what they actually feel, as they are generally consumed by the feeling and just reacting. They are even less aware of how they feel about what they are feeling. This second feeling, however, is usually an extremely important part of the dynamic, as it reflects a person's relationship with the first feeling. In fact, it is frequently what is creating or sustaining a particular CRASH State. Imagine if somebody says, "I feel frustrated," and you ask, "Well, how do you feel about feeling frustrated?" They say, "I feel ashamed that I feel frustrated. I feel like that I shouldn't be that way."

Similarly, if somebody says, "I feel afraid," you may ask, "Well, how do you feel about feeling afraid?" When people are afraid of their own fear, it very quickly becomes panic. "I'm afraid, and then I'm afraid that I'm afraid." In contrast, the pilot from the Miracle on the Hudson example claimed that he been more afraid for his life during the incident yet was able to hold that fear from a place of deeper calm.

A colleague of Robert's, transformational teacher and coach Richard Moss, often poses a very interesting question when somebody he is working with says they're afraid. He asks, *"Is your fear safe inside of you?"* This is a powerful question, because it is very often our relationship to a particular feeling that determines whether it's going to be a problem or not.

In the Holding Difficult Feelings process, we are going to find a place where we meet an obstacle as we move into action that triggers a difficult feeling or emotional response which creates some type of CRASH. The first thing we are going to do when we encounter that CRASH is to slow down, pause, breathe, and center. Then, we'll welcome that response and explore the question, "So, how do you feel?" and bring awareness to the feeling.

Then we're going to ask a second question which is, "How do you feel about feeling that way?" That's often likely to be something that we have not really brought our awareness to before. Of course, when we engage that second feeling, we are also going to slow down, pause, breathe, center, and welcome it. As we reduce the CRASH associated with these feelings, we are able to more easily explore and understand their positive intentions.

Then we're going to go back to our COACH State and, holding both of those feelings, connect to our larger self and find: "What resources can I bring?" Then we're going to bring those resources, first to the second feeling, and then to the first feeling. Connecting these feelings to new resources in a COACH state will inevitably bring a transformation in the way that they are expressed.

The simple summary of the prototype for *Holding Difficult Feelings* is, when we meet an obstacle, we explore:

1. "How do you feel?"

2. "How do you feel about feeling that way?"

3. From COACH State, "What resources do you need to be able to hold both of those feelings in a way that their expression can be transformed into something more aligned with your intention?"

As an illustration, the following is a transcript of a demonstration of *Holding Difficult Feelings* that Robert did as part of a virtual training course.

Demonstration of Holding Difficult Feelings

Helen: *Hello. I'm Helen and I'm really grateful for being this demo subject.*

Robert: *I am looking forward to doing some interesting and useful work together. I can see that you're already standing, which is great. Why don't we just do a little bit of COACH State Tai Chi together—centering, opening, being alert, aware, connect to the cognitive intelligence in the head, the emotional intelligence in the heart and the intuition in the belly.* [Robert and Helen make the COACH State Tai Chi gestures together.]

Helen, is there anything else you would like to add that helps you get into a strong COACH State?

Helen: *For myself, I can see the image of myself in the forest, standing in the moss, and there are a lot of pine trees. I can see this trunk of the pine tree. It gets me grounded.*

Robert: *Great. If you take that image of the forest and that tree, what do you feel is the level of your COACH State right now, from zero to ten?*

Helen: *Ten.*

Robert: *Ten? Great. From this COACH State, let's look at what your intention is. What is it that you are really wanting to create?*

Helen: *I have my club. I have mostly created it. It's a club for women. I work with women who struggle with giving birth to a child.*

Robert: *Okay. Great.*

Helen: *This club is about different topics. It is about more than just getting pregnant. It's about how to carry a baby, how to give birth, and how do you deal with this newborn child. How do you help to bring up this child as a healthy person psychologically? It is also a club for women that might need help in their family life, partnership, and self-realization.*

Robert: *And what is your intention with respect to this club? What is it that you really are wanting to bring or create? I can imagine also in today's challenging world, there's probably a lot of things that are really difficult for a pregnant woman. What do you most want to create?*

Helen: *By the end of this year, I want to have more than twenty-thousand participants in my club. I want not just me, but other specialists giving talks and webinars in this club.*

Robert: *That's great. By the way, that's what we would call an "**ambition.**" It's your ambition, to help twenty-thousand people and attract other specialists. Now, let's see if we can put that into five words. How would you express this intention if you were going to just do it in five words?*

Helen: *I have twenty-thousand participants in my club by the end of this year.*

Robert: *Great. What would be your gesture?*

Helen: [Pumps both fists in front of her and then raises them over her head.] *Yes!!*

Robert: [Mirrors the gesture.] *Yes! And what would be your image for that? What picture do you have of that intention?*

Helen: *I can feel that this is a community and that we feel each other. I can support them, and we hug each other. They feel as a community. I picture a big group of people giving each other hugs.*

Robert: *Okay, great, big hugs. Let's put them all together. You see that image and then you're going to make your gesture and say that intention out loud. So, my intention is . . .*

Helen: *My intention is to have twenty-thousand participants by December, and I've managed to do this.* [Pumps both fists in front of her and then raises them over her head.]

Robert: *Great. Really breathe that intention in. And check, how strongly do you feel connected to that intention right now? Where in your body do you feel that intention most? Zero to ten, how strongly do you feel that?*

Helen: *It is in my heart, and it's ten.*

Robert: *You got a lot of tens. Wow. This is really clearly a big, outer game goal. To create that outer game, your inner game will be really important. As we go to your generative state,*

which is where you're connected to your center, COACH State, and intention, what other resources are important to support you? Who or what from your field of resources can really be there to help you to achieve this intention?

Helen: *I have this resource, that's my team, and the participants that have already joined. I have this gesture that I'm kind of spreading it all around.* [Moves her hands and arms out from her body.]

Robert: [Mirrors the gesture.] *Wow. That's got a lot of energy. I love that.*

Helen: [Moves her hands and arms more vigorously and smiles broadly.] *I'm kind of splashing it around.*

Robert: [Mirrors the gesture.] *How strongly can you feel connected to this resource?*

Helen: *It's like ten again.*

Robert: *Wow, okay. I can tell you, for that big ambition, it's going to be good to have tens. Helen, just one more thing before we start to move into action and look for some of these obstacles. I think what will be also really helpful is that we have that presence of your larger self that comes from having what we are calling a "second skin." To reach that big ambition and intention, you need to stay in the best version of yourself. Perhaps you can feel the presence of your second skin where there's a sense of security, but also a space for you. This larger self is also connected to your field of resources.* [Robert and Helen make sculpting gestures around their bodies.]

Great. Our next step is going to be to lay out a timeline and the steps that you need to take as you move into action. What we want to do is to find where you're going to meet some challenges where it could be difficult for you to stay in COACH

State. As you think of really moving into action, to create this club of twenty-thousand people and all these specialists, where do you anticipate some of the biggest obstacles and challenges for you?

Helen: *It's about scaling up. When more people are coming, I have this fear that I wouldn't be able to hold it, that I won't have enough energy to contain it. Me, as a leader, because I would attract all this attention, these twenty-thousand pairs of eyes would look at me and watch me.*

Robert: *That makes sense. Let's explore that together. What I'm going to invite you to do is to take two steps forward and put yourself into that situation. You're scaling up. It is getting bigger, there are all these eyes on you. We take the two steps. You put yourself there.* [Helen takes two steps forward.] *It's scaling up. As the leader, it's requiring even more energy. There are all these eyes on you. Put yourself there. See what you see, hear what you hear, feel what you feel. We're noticing any places where you begin to meet some kind of inner obstacle. And again, our first question here is, "What do you feel?"*

Helen: *It's fear and confusion of some kind. I can feel it in my belly and up here* [clasps her hands across her upper chest]. *It's like a metal strip somewhere around here.*

Robert: *So interesting.* [Mirrors the gesture.] *Fear, and you also said confusion. So, let's first take a moment, slow down, pause, breathe, center.* [Robert makes the four gestures and Helen mirrors him.] *And as we meet this fear and this confusion, we say, "That's interesting, I'm sure it makes sense. There's something there that's needing to be held, heard, maybe healed. Welcome."*

Helen: *Welcome.*

Robert: *If we seek to understand this fear and confusion, what is the positive intention? What is it trying to do for you?*

Helen: *Protect me.*

Robert: *Yes. That's interesting. That's good to know. That's why we can say, "Welcome." It's good to be protected.*

Helen: *I can say, "Welcome," to this.*

Robert: *Now Helen, let's take a step back from this fear and confusion.* [Helen takes a step back.] *When you have that fear and confusion, how do you typically feel about it? And how do you feel about yourself when you are afraid and confused?*

Helen: *I don't like it. I freeze up and try to control it. I become rigid and controlling.* [Closes her hand into tight fists and holds them in front of her.]

Robert: [Mirrors the gesture.] *Rigid and controlling. I'm sure that makes sense as well. There's something here that is also needing to be held, heard, and possibly healed. Welcome.*

Helen: *Welcome.* [Her fists begin to relax.]

Robert: *We can also look at what's the positive intention of this second feeling.*

Helen: *Some kind of a pause. It's when you have to think to get all your thoughts, to be ready to move to the next steps.*

Robert: *Gathering your thoughts and getting ready to move to the next steps. That, like protection is also important. Welcome.*

Helen: *Welcome.*

Robert: *So now, Helen, let's take a step back from that. In front of you, so you can see, there's the first feeling, the fear, and the confusion.* [Clasps his hands across his chest.] *The second feeling, which is this freezing and trying to control.* [Makes tight fists with his hands.] *Here in this third place, we're going to come back to COACH State and reconnect to your intention, and your resources. Then, that second skin. Many leaders*

have told me about how valuable and powerful they found it to have a second skin because you're the focus of so much energy from a bigger field. Now, the question here is for you is, when you can stay connected to your resources and to this larger you, what resource comes to you that allows you to hold these other two feelings? The fear and confusion and the freezing up and controlling; what resource can you bring to them?*

Helen: [Begins to move her hands and arms in circles in front of her.] *To keep going. I feel like I'm swimming.*

Robert: [Mirrors the gesture.] *Yes.*

Helen: [Continues to repeat the gesture.] *I like to swim. It helps me to think and to find new solutions.*

Robert: *Fantastic.* [Mirrors the movement.] *Always remember too, you have your forest, and you have your pine tree. Now you can add swimming.*

Helen: [Continues to repeat the gesture and smiles broadly.]

Robert: *Great. Now, Helen, the next thing we're going to do is bring these resources and step forward to the place where there's been the freezing and controlling.* [Helen steps forward continuing to make the circular movement with her hands and arms.] *And we're honoring the positive intention of this feeling which was, "to gather your thoughts and get ready to move to the next steps." It can be interesting to move back and forth between those tightly closed fists and your swimming motion.* [Helen closes her fists and then makes the swimming motion several times.] *I'm curious, what happens to that feeling and all the energy of that feeling when you bring these resources?*

Helen: *Something has changed. I realized that this freezing is some kind of a pause for me that I need to stop and to think things over; to calm down, center myself. And then I am able to find the proper solution. When I have all these resources my body reacts in a different way. It doesn't just freeze up. It relaxes and calms itself down.*

Robert: *Fantastic.*

Helen: *I just felt it this way. I saw there is a pause, but not as freezing.*

Robert: *Yes, a pause versus a freezing. Pausing, relaxing, calming down. Now we can then take a step to the first feeling again.* [Helen takes a step forward.] *And we can bring your resources* [makes a swimming gesture] *here to this fear and this confusion and its intention of protection. As you move between that metal strip and your swimming gesture, notice what happens to the fear and confusion.*

Helen: [Helen moves between clasping her hands across her chest and making her swimming gesture several times.] *My belly relaxes. I have less of this confusion and no fear.*

Robert: *What happens to that energy?*

Helen: *It expands. It just expands.*

Robert: *Now, Helen, as you are there with these new resources, once again really bring your attention back to the outer game, the twenty-thousand eyes looking at you. The business is scaling up. When you really go back to that same outer game but with these new resources in your inner game, what is different and what becomes possible for you now?*

Helen: *I can feel how my hands get bigger. I feel energy coming out from my belly and it expands. I feel a huge sense of potential.*

Robert: *It's really amazing also, Helen, because when I look at you, I just see a bigger you. I really see this humble authority of a true leader. That's something that you will also project out to the others in your club, as well. And this is where the very important issue of practice comes in. This is such a great example because you're like the pilot of that airplane. You're the leader of this club. The pilot said the thing that helped him from when he encountered this very crucial situation that could have been a disaster was that he had practiced. So, I'm curious, what could be something, a practice, that you could do regularly, that helps you as you go forward as you grow your club over these coming months? What will you do to make sure that you can stay connected to these resources of your inner game?*

Helen: *I will swim, meditate, do the COACH State Tai Chi and four movements of slowing down, pausing, breathing, and centering. I will also spend time in the forest with my pine tree and let myself to find these new ideas and plans, and how to proceed and go further.*

Robert: *You know what? If I was there, I would high-five you and say, "Yes, you can!"* [Makes a high five gesture.]

Helen: [Makes a high five gesture and smiles broadly.]

Robert: *Thank you, Helen. I am glad to know you're doing something so important for our world and for our future. I honor that vision and ambition for you. Before we end, is there anything that you want to share that was particularly either useful or helpful for this practice?*

Helen: *For me, it is very important to understand what resources these obstacles bring me. There's fear and freezing. I realized that this freezing is a magnificent resource of being able to slow down, stop, and not act in a CRASH State. When the fear comes, I will just engage my resources and let the fear transform into flow and to meet other resources.*

Robert: *Great. Thank you so much. It's been a real pleasure.*

Helen: *Thank you too. It really greatly helped.*

Detailed Summary of the Process

The following is a detailed summary of the steps of the *Holding Difficult Feelings* process.

1. Identify a challenging situation in which you experience a difficult feeling that you are not able to hold and, consequently, brings you into an unresourceful (CRASH) State. Experience that feeling and the associated sensations and allow your body to express it as gesture or movement. Bring acknowledgment and awareness to the feelings and sensations without any attempt to change, analyze or explain them.

2. Step back from the location in which you were experiencing this difficult feeling and reflect upon the you who is experiencing the difficult feelings. How do you feel about those difficult feelings? How do you feel about yourself for feeling them? What is your relationship with those feelings and with yourself when you are feeling them? There may be a number of feelings about the first feeling (shame, guilt, despair, anger, helplessness, etc.). Allow your body to express these feelings as a gesture or movement as well. As in the previous step, bring acknowledgment and awareness to these feelings and sensations without judgment or any attempt to change them.

3. Now step back to a third location, shift your state by turning around, moving your body, shaking your arms and legs, etc. Take the time necessary to put yourself into a resourceful state in which you are centered, open, awake and connected to a field of resources that is

bigger than you. What resources (e.g., trust, acceptance, curiosity, strength, love, etc.) could help you to hold the second set of feelings more lovingly, respectfully and resourcefully? Open to the larger field and allow yourself to receive the resources without thinking about it. Notice what emerges from the field. It may come in the form of images, symbols, feelings, etc.

4. Bring the resources that have emerged from the field fully into your body and being. (If you need to, you can facilitate this by finding reference experiences for these resources and reliving them as fully as you can.) Find a symbol and a gesture or movement (somatic model) that expresses these resources and brings them present in your body. Allow the energy of these resources to flow fully through you both from the field and into the field around you.

5. With these resources fully present in your body, return to the second location (the feelings about the feelings). Don't attempt to change anything. Just hold the feelings and responses associated with the second location within the larger field of the resources. Make the gesture and movement associated with the resources you have received in the previous step. Notice what shifts in your perception and attitude toward the second set of feelings.

6. Now step into the location in which you placed the original difficult feelings and bring with you the resources you have identified. Again, don't attempt to change anything. Just hold the difficult feelings and responses within the larger field of the resources. Make the gesture and movement associated with the resources you have received. How do you feel now about those difficult feelings? What changes in your ability to be with those difficult feelings?

Call upon your resources.

Let the difficult feeling transform.

Set up ways to practice.

Building a Belief Bridge

As we have established in the previous volumes of Generative Coaching, obstacles come in many different forms. Sometimes they're challenging emotions. Other times they are critical voices. They also frequently come in the form of limiting beliefs. We refer to some types of limiting beliefs as "thought viruses," which basically means that it's a thought that can infect us and create damaging effects, similar to a computer virus or a biological virus. In this section, we will be exploring some possible ways of transforming limiting beliefs and thought viruses.

Limiting Beliefs

In Chapter 4, we established that the basic beliefs needed for generative change included things like, it is important, it's possible, it's appropriate, I'm capable, I deserve it and I have permission and support. The most common limiting beliefs are essentially the opposites of those. In fact, we can summarize the most common limiting beliefs as those that create hopelessness, helplessness, and worthlessness.

Hopelessness comes from the belief that it is not possible to achieve my intention. *Helplessness* results from the belief that I am powerless or not capable to achieve my intention (even if it possible). *Worthlessness* is the consequence of the belief that I'm not good enough. I don't have value. I don't deserve it. These are often the kind of barriers that we're going to meet when we are starting to move into action, though, of course, they can come up at any point in the coaching process.

What we call a *"belief barrier"* often starts as a thought but becomes something more than just a thought. Belief barriers are thoughts that create either fear about the future or doubt about ourselves. They interfere with our sense of confidence, our sense of hope and/or our sense of self-esteem.

Thought Viruses

There are two ways that we build a belief. One is through our own experience. I try something and it doesn't work, or it does work, and I begin to develop a generalization as a result my experience. But some beliefs, we pick up from other people. We don't learn them ourselves. They come from the field if you will. We hear them or learn them from our parents, our culture, our friends, the media, etc. Some of these beliefs are positive and helpful. Others are potentially harmful and damaging.

When some calls another person "stupid" or "fat" or "ugly" or "crazy," it is a generalization that is not being made by the person who is receiving the statements. They are coming from the other person. In a sense, the receiver is being potentially "infected" by the other person. If the receiver is in a CRASH State and they hear these words, there can be a kind of strange resonance. They feel badly and somebody saying something like that somehow confirms that feeling, so they start to believe it. Some beliefs don't even come verbally. Somebody doesn't necessarily have to say something, but the way that they react makes another person feel, "I've done something wrong," or "This is crazy." These types of generalizations will resonate with some CRASH State and then, later on, they create the CRASH.

Similar to a physical virus, if your body is healthy and strong and you have immunity, you could be around the virus and not pick it up. Either (a) you don't get the virus; it doesn't affect you; or (b) your body is able to heal itself quickly. The exact same virus can be harmful or even deadly for people are already ill or have a compromised immune system. Analogously, a CRASH State is a type of compromised psychological state. In a COACH State, a person has greater immunity to self-limiting generalizations or "thought viruses." And, in this section, we would like to show a couple of ways that we can support ourselves and our clients to develop such immunity to thought viruses.

Belief Barriers and Belief Bridges

The first way we're going to do this is by working to create a "belief bridge." A belief bridge connects us to a higher-level belief that immunizes us to the limiting belief. It resonates with deeper and more resourceful experiences than those activated by the limiting belief and takes us to something more fundamental. When that happens, the limiting belief no longer has the same damaging effect.

As shown in the following diagram, a *belief barrier* is a generalization that stops us from being able to bring some resourceful response to a particular context.

A *belief bridge* helps us to get beyond and transform the belief barrier by "outframing" it. *Outframing* involves establishing a larger frame of reference that alters the meaning and impact of a limiting belief. A belief bridge is a belief that honors the positive intention of the belief barrier and at the same time creates a larger perspective that helps the person reconnect to their intention (**Vision, Mission, Ambition, Role**) and their bigger field of resources.

Thus, a belief bridge very often takes the form of a belief statement about identity, purpose or the connection to something beyond oneself.

One way to build a belief bridge is to do a type of "thought experiment" in which you project yourself into the future to where you have already transcended the barrier and look back at how you did that. Going into the future and looking back, you ask yourself, "How have I transformed this barrier? What belief moved me beyond this barrier?" As you do, bring your focus to the highest levels of the change pyramid (identity and purpose.)

Basic Prototype for Building a Belief Bridge

1. Think of a challenging situation in which it is difficult for you to bring your intention into action. Create a physical location for it on your timeline (*storyboard*) and put yourself into that situation. Bring awareness to how you experience the situation and the barrier; seeing what you see, hearing what you hear and feeling what you feel. Identify where in your body and how you experience the CRASH associated with the barrier.

2. *"Taste the poison"*—Holding the difficult feelings associated with the barrier, explore the limiting belief, or thought virus that is creating the CRASH. Identify the thoughts that accompany and/or produce the CRASH State.

3. *"Thought experiment"*—Once you have identified the belief barrier, return to COACH State and, on your timeline, step into your future, going beyond the barrier to the experience of being fully connected to your field of resources and having achieved your intention. Using your imagination, explore the questions, "Going into the future and now looking back, how have I transformed this barrier? What belief moved me beyond this barrier?" Bring your focus to empowering beliefs related to your *identity* and *purpose*.

4. Breathe the belief associated with the "belief bridge" into your **head**, **heart**, and **gut**. Create a *somatic model* for the belief bridge.

5. Return to the present on your timeline bringing the *belief bridge* and its *somatic model*. Step back into the challenging situation, maintaining your attention on the belief bridge. Notice how it transcends and transforms the *belief barrier*.

The following is a transcript of a demonstration of *Building a Belief Bridge* that Robert did as part of a virtual training course.

Demonstration for Building a Belief Bridge

COACH State Tai-Chi

Rachel: Hello. My name is Rachel. I'm a medical doctor and psychotherapist.

Robert: Hi Rachel, welcome. Let's begin with a little COACH State Tai Chi. Centering, opening, awakening, connecting, and holding a resourceful field between us. [Robert and Rachel go through the COACH State Tai Chi movements together.] Rachel, is there anything else that you find especially helpful for you to get to your COACH State?

Rachel: When they told me that I would be a demo subject, I was afraid that I wouldn't be able to find my COACH State. I was so worried. Then I felt my vertical channel that comes to my body from above me going through my spine and down to my legs. And I tell myself that the strength of the universe is inside me.

Robert: Wonderful. When you do that, and when you tell yourself that, what happens inside?

Rachel: I can see, and I can feel a ray of light in me.

Robert: Wow, I can see that ray of light in you right now Rachel. On a scale of zero to ten, what would you say now your COACH State is?

Rachel: I would say eight.

Robert: Great. Then let's move to Step 2. What is your intention? What is it that you would like to create?

Rachel: I've been working as a psychotherapist for the past twenty years, and I really feel that that is my mission. I'm totally into that. I've been working offline all this time but, especially with all of the changes going on in the world, I feel that I need to move online.

Robert: So, if we were going to put your intention into five words, how would you say it?

Rachel: The syntax is wrong but, to thousands of people, I bring harmony online. How do I say that? It kind of sounds strange. I bring transformation to thousands of people regardless, offline, or online.

Robert: Find the way you can say that and really feel, "Yeah, that's what I want to do. That is what I want to create." Say it one more time and also begin to find your somatic model for that.

Rachel: I help thousands of people. [Opens arms out widely from her upper chest.] I help thousands of people. [Repeats the gesture.]

Robert: Yes, wonderful. [Mirrors the gesture.] I see that there's a nice breath when you said that. When you said that [breathes] I feel like it comes a little bit more resonant in your heart and in your belly. What happens to you when you say that?

Rachel: I can feel this trembling and this inspiration. If I could really help these thousands of people, that would be true happiness.

Robert: Wonderful. What image do you have of this when you say that and make that gesture?

Rachel: I have an image from an old fairy tale in which, when the main female character moves one hand from her sleeve, there is a lake, and from other sleeve there are white swans. [Opens arms out widely from her chest and smiles broadly.]

Robert: Wonderful. It gives me shivers. Rachel, as we connect to your center and you connect to this intention, and open to your field of resources, which resources are you going to need to really make this intention become a reality?

Rachel: I would need a lot of motivation and I would need a lot of inspiration to sustain myself.

Robert: As you hold your intention, and you connect to your center, if you open to your field of resources, who or what comes to you as a support or help for your motivation and inspiration?

Rachel: It's my family.

Robert: Where do you feel the presence of your family around you? Are they within you, behind you, next to you?

Rachel: I feel surrounded with the care that I receive from my husband. I can feel it around me.

Robert: When you feel that all around you, what happens inside of you? What do you become aware of?

Rachel: I feel better. It's easier for me.

Robert: That's good to know. One last thing, I remember that before we start to move into action, we have previously worked with this notion of a second skin. Were you able to create your second skin?

Rachel: Yes. It's really important to have this second skin because I take everything personally close to my heart. I'm really sensitive.

Robert: It's important to be able to stay sensitive because that's part of how you help people, but it's also important to stay protected and safe.

Rachel: Yeah, that's really important. I need to feel this sense of protection. [Rachel gestures as if sculpting a second skin around her body.]

Robert: Great. Now we are ready to start moving into action and searching for any belief barriers. What I'd like to invite you to do, Rachel, is really imagine, if you start to step forward into your storyboard on the timeline, is there any place where you meet a barrier? Is there anything that stops you from taking action?

Rachel: [Takes a step and hesitates.] *Yes. I am meeting quite a bit of fear.* [Shoulders become tense and breathing shallows.]

Robert: Let's take a moment and slow down, pause, breath and center. [Robert and Rachel make the four gestures together.] *Let's first hold and welcome that fear. I am sure that, with such big intention, it makes sense.*

Rachel: Welcome.

Robert: Then let's bring our attention to what is creating that fear and "taste the poison." What is the belief that is producing this fear and this barrier?

Rachel: What if that would be so difficult that I wouldn't be able to come through? Will I feel strong enough to do all that? That's so much. I'm not sure that I would be able to do all of that.

Robert: Again, let's slow down, pause, breath, center, and welcome those thoughts. [Robert and Rachel make the four gestures together.] *It's essentially relating to this belief that, "Maybe, I'm not capable. Maybe, I can't do it."*

Rachel:Yes. It is too much. I am not capable to manage it all.

Robert: So, the belief, "It's too much. You are not capable to manage it all." We want to say to that, "Welcome. I'm sure it makes sense. That needs to be heard and held." So instead of trying to ignore it, we want to really listen to it, especially to its positive intention. What is the positive intention of this belief? What is it trying to do for you?

Rachel: The positive intention is to take care of me, to protect me. If I would be going toward this intention, wouldn't it interfere? Wouldn't it endanger my relation to myself, to my health, to my children, to my husband? What if this work would totally overflow and fill all my life?

Robert: *That makes sense. This belief is here to protect the ecology of your holon. It's a very important part of your team. Welcome.*

Rachel: *Welcome.*

Robert: *Now, as we really honor that positive intention of the barrier, I would like to invite you to take a step into the future where you are helping thousands of people and, at the same time, respecting the ecology of your holon.* [Robert and Rachel take a step forward, beyond the location of the belief barrier.] *This is what aesthetic intelligence is all about. Make this thought experiment, "If I could help thousands of people in a way that was okay for me, for my children, for my husband, for my health, what would that be like? If it were possible and I was capable, what would that be like?" As you do, stay connected to your center, your intention, that ray of light that lets you know that the strength of the universe is within you, and you have your second skin with you, and you are surrounded by the care of your husband and your family.*

Rachel: [Smiles broadly.] *Oh, that's so great. Then it goes with ease and, like, all by itself. It is like when I am working with my clients, I don't have to prepare. I don't have to do anything special. It's easy. I can just see this patient and the process just flows. I know how to help them find this ecology in their own lives. The universe guides me. I am connected to something bigger than me.*

Robert: *Awesome. It really feels to me like you are talking about the same thing Milton Erickson meant when he referred to the* "creative unconscious." *It sounds like, in the future, to reach these thousands of people online, you are able to support yourself with the same wisdom you provide your clients.*

Rachel: *Yes. Yes,* [Smiling] *I have the capability. I just need to apply it to me!*

Robert: So, now here's the next question. From the future now looking back . . . how have you transformed that barrier? [Robert and Rachel turn to look back from the future location.] What belief moved you beyond that barrier that "it's too much, and you are not capable to manage it all?"

Rachel: It is something like: "I can do the same thing for me that I do for my clients. When I connect to the strength and wisdom of the universe, everything is possible." It is like what you say about the whole being in every part. When I let the universe guide me, everything is possible. I just have to slow down and listen and go step by step. Ten can turn into ten thousand.

Robert: So, "When I let the wisdom of the universe guide me, everything is possible, step by step." Where do you feel and experience this belief most in your body?

Rachel: In my belly.

Robert: Let's breathe with that in the belly. That belief, "When I let the universe guide me, everything is possible, step by step." What would be your somatic model for this belief?

Rachel: When I let the wisdom of the universe guide me, everything is possible, step by step. [Lifts her arms and hands above her head and brings them down to her heart, then opens them out in front of her, moving one in front of the other.]

Robert: When I let the wisdom of the universe guide me, everything is possible, step by step. [Mirrors the gesture.]

Rachel: When I let the wisdom of the universe guide me, everything is possible, step by step. [Repeats the gesture.]

Robert: Any image that goes with this? [Mirrors the gesture.]

Rachel: [Repeats the gesture. Smiles broadly.] *I can see a lot of sparkling eyes and happy faces.*

Robert: I like that. Now our last step, Rachel, is we're going to take this belief and this somatic model and this image, and step back to the present. We bring that belief bridge from the future with you. [Robert and Rachel step back to the present location.] *So, in addition to the resource of your family around you and your second skin, you also now have, very deep in the belly, this belief that, "When I let the universe guide me, everything is possible, step by step," and the image of those sparkling eyes and your gesture.* [Lifts his arms and hands above his head and brings them down to his heart, then opens them out in front of him, moving one in front of the other.] *So, as you take that step into action and you meet that belief or that thought, "Well what if I can't, what if it's too much?" what happens?*

Rachel: [Mirrors the gesture and steps forward into the location of the belief barrier.] *I will listen to my body. I'll keep track of whether I am in a good, resourceful state. I feel that I always have this energy within me that I can share it with my clients, my husband, my family, and myself. And I can restore it and recharge it, so it would never end.*

Robert: Yes. And I just want to say that Steve and I share your vision. Obviously, this is what we do in the world. We want to help thousands of people with our work on generative change and generative coaching. And, having that sense of mission and seeing all those sparkling eyes, as you said, really gives almost infinite energy. We are also careful to take care of ourselves, to take care of our relationships and our families. So, I can tell you from my own experience, it is possible to help thousands of people and stay healthy and in an ecological balance. And it requires, exactly as you've been doing, to really welcome, and listen to those parts of you that want to protect you. The wonderful thing is, now, instead of stopping you, that becomes part of your team.

Rachel: [Smiles broadly.] *Thank you. I am sure I can do it now!*

Robert: So, obviously, Rachel, I just want to say, I send you my full support. I am sure thousands of people need your help.

Rachel: I want to thank you, Robert, because I consider our today's conversation as a blessing. That's really important for me. Thank you

Building a Belief Bridge

Review of the Steps for Building a Belief Bridge

To review, we start with Step 1, COACH State. Then, Step 2, the intention. After that, Step 3, the field of resources needed to support achieving that intention. Now, the next question is, "As I start moving into action, where do I meet any possible belief barriers?" This is going into the Critic phase. The simple question that I asked Rachel was: "What stops you? What stops you from taking action?" So, it is a very simple question but, often, a very useful and powerful question. That's where we're going to slow down, pause, breathe, and center. We are going to welcome whatever that obstacle is and explore what limiting belief is associated with it. Of course, even a very limiting sounding belief has a positive intention. Many times, it is about protection, as we observed in the demonstration with Rachel.

Once we identify and acknowledge the positive intention of this *belief barrier*, then we are going to do this thought experiment. Using our timeline, we step into the future beyond the barrier and act "as if" we are able to achieve our intention while still honoring the positive intention of the barrier. The simple coaching question is, "If you put yourself into the future, as if you could transcend or transform the barrier, what would it be like? In this future now looking back, what is the belief that has taken you beyond that barrier?" Then, of course, if we connect that question, that thought experiment, to the generative state and to all our resources, including our second skin, many new possibilities will come up.

The important thing is that we are not ignoring the limiting belief that's trying to protect us. We are actually honoring its positive intention and exploring other possibilities. I find the frame of "thought experiment" really helpful at this stage because it makes it clear that it is an exploration and consequently reduces resistance.

As we could see in Rachel's example, belief bridges are often a belief statement that connects us to something bigger than ourselves. Her belief, "When I let the wisdom of the universe guide me, everything is possible, step by step," connected her to the top of the levels pyramid.

Once we have identified the new belief, we can breathe it into the body (head, heart and gut) and bring the *belief bridge*, and the *somatic model* and images that go with it, back to our present state. And here we realize that the barrier, even if the thought is there, is not a barrier anymore because it's a useful part of our team. Instead of being a barrier, it becomes a resource.

Of course, the next step is to reinforce the actions and resources necessary to reach the intention through some type of practice. And that is what we will focus on in the next chapter.

ANTONIO MEZA

Practice means to perform, over and over again in the face of all obstacles, some act of vision, of faith, of desire. Practice is a means of inviting the perfection desired.

We learn by practice. Whether it means to learn to dance by practicing dancing or to learn to live by practicing living, the principles are the same. One becomes in some area an athlete of God.

– Martha Graham

Chapter 7

Step 6
Practices for Deepening the Changes

The final step of the Generative Coaching process involves establishing practices that deepen and sustain the changes begun during the actual coaching session. The importance of this step cannot be over emphasized. As the saying from Papua New Guinea goes, "Knowledge is only a rumor until it's in the muscle." And practice is the way that you get something in the muscle.

Sometimes we get questions about how much someone needs to practice something for it to make a difference. Interestingly, all of the studies on muscle memory say that it takes about roughly twenty-one days of consistent practice to internalize a new behavior, such as a golf swing or a dance routine. So, this provides us with an interesting kind of a standard. It means that it probably takes at least a good three weeks of regular practice before something really becomes automatic. That is one of the reasons that we ask our clients to commit to at least thirty minutes of practice per day if they really want to change. We, as the coach, are working with our coachees to try to find a high leverage practice—something that they can do in an ongoing, repeating way to really make something either stronger or more sustainable.

We may assign practices for any one of the steps of the Generative Coaching process. The types of practices we assign are often simplified versions of one of the prototypes that we have used in the coaching session. The following are some examples of possible practices relating to the various steps of Generative Coaching.

Practices for Accessing and Deepening COACH State

An important goal of all generative change work is to help clients develop a strong COACH State as a baseline state. In addition to the methods provided in the first two volumes of *Generative Coaching*, we presented several ways in this book to help coachees access a COACH State and to deepen it such as, the *Active Centering* exercises, *COACH State Tai Chi* and the process of *Finding your Center*. We will frequently encourage coachees to include versions of Active Centering or COACH State Tai Chi as part of a daily practice. Reconnecting with key somatic anchors, like the four presented in the previous chapter (slow down, pause, breathe, center), or those created during processes like *Finding Your Center* presented in **Chapter 2**, is also a useful practice.

There can be many creative ways to incorporate these practices in an ongoing way. One of Robert's coachees, a very successful Silicon Valley entrepreneur, does a whole routine of movements in the shower every morning to prepare for his day. Robert and his wife Deborah will often practice "subway surfing" when they are on the Paris Metro by standing in the subway car while it is moving without holding on to anything. This is an excellent natural form of Active Centering. We often encourage our clients to spontaneously seek natural practice situations like this. Even just looking for them brings an ongoing awareness to the quality of one's ongoing state.

Another simple but powerful practice for **Step 1** of the Generative Coaching process is to have coachees keep track of their average COACH State on a daily basis in a journal or notebook. A frequent question we will ask clients as we begin a session is, "On a scale of zero to ten, what has been your average COACH State since our last session?" If it has been below seven, regardless of the external challenges the person has faced, it indicates that there is still some significant work that can be done to bolster their ability to recover and sustain a good level of COACH State.

A simple worksheet, like the following, can be provided to help the coachee keep track of their COACH State, which also promotes the inner game skills of self-awareness, self-modeling and self-calibration. The coach and coachee select the period to check, which could be hours, days or weeks.

What has been your average COACH State?

Period 01

Period 02

Period 03

Period 04

Practices for Connecting to Intentions

The coachee's intention is the focus and purpose of all Generative Coaching activity. Thus, having practices that help the coachee keep their attention centered on their intention can be very important. There can be many distractions that cause people to lose sight of what they are actually wanting to create in their lives.

Making sure that coachees are staying connected to their intentions in an ongoing way after a coaching session is necessary for the session to have a useful effect. One way to do that is a practice using what we call the *"More of/Less of" Worksheet*. The worksheet consists of a simple chart that can either be given to coachees, or which they can create themselves on a piece of paper or in a journal. The chart involves writing the five words of the intention at the top of the page and then creating two columns relating to behaviors to do "more of" or "less of" in order to reach the intention.

Intention: ____

Behaviors

More of	*Less of*
________________________	________________________
________________________	________________________
________________________	________________________
________________________	________________________
________________________	________________________

For example, in the demonstration in chapter 4, Martha expressed the intention to *take care of herself, trust herself and love herself* as a balance to the increasing responsibilities she had to care for others. The following is an example of a *"More of/Less of" Worksheet* that she might fill out as part of an ongoing practice.

Intention: Take care of myself, trust myself, love myself

Behaviors

More of	*Less of*
Making time for myself	Putting myself second
Being like a cat	Taking things so seriously
Using moisturizing cream	Ignoring my health and mood
Running up the stairs and feeeling my strong legs	Sitting and feeling sorry for myself

Once such a chart is filled in, coachees would check it on, optimally, in a daily basis but minimally every few days, and potentially add other behaviors to do more of and less of as they become more in touch with the realities and challenges of their situations.

Of course, it is important that coachees don't just abstractly think about their intentions. A key element of the practice would involve them projecting themselves into their future and engaging multiple intelligences (words, images, somatic models, metaphors, etc.). And a good check would be the *future of no regrets test*—"If I **do not** do more of X and less of Y will I regret it today, tomorrow, next week, next month, next year, etc.?"

Another useful practice for **Step 2** of the Generative Coaching process is to create concrete reminders of the intention. We will frequently invite coachees to make signs, and put them up around their homes and offices. For instance, in Martha's case, she might create signs for her living and working environments with messages like, "If I was taking care of myself right now, what would I be doing?" "How would I act if I trusted?" "What is Love asking of me?"

Practices for Developing and Deepening a Generative State

The key to developing and deepening a generative state is clearly the capacity to stay connected to our center, our intention and our field of resources. In *Generative Coaching Volume 1* (p. 180) we presented the process of *Creating Resource Anchors* as a type of "preparation practice." *Anchoring* refers to the process of associating an internal response with some environmental or mental trigger, so that the response may be quickly re-accessed.

The process of anchoring can be used to help people remember and gain access to their inner resources. A remembered picture may become an anchor for a particular internal feeling, for instance. A particular gesture or an article of clothing can become an anchor for an inner state such as confidence. A voice tone may become an anchor for a state of excitement or determination. A person may consciously choose to establish and retrigger these associations for him or herself. Used in this way, an anchor becomes a tool for self-empowerment.

As a practice, the process of anchoring can be applied by coachees to create cues or triggers to remind themselves of their goals and their resources. A key assumption of generative change work is that coachees have the resources they need, within their larger field of resources, to make positive changes and get what they want. Frequently, though, they forget or fail to connect with those resources at times when they most need them. Creating anchors for those resources greatly increases the chance that they will be able to have access to the right resource at the right time.

When working with some of our business clients, we will jokingly say that "whoever has the most anchors wins." By "winning" in this case, we don't mean making someone else lose but rather be able to maintain a generative state and remain connected to our field of resources, no matter what happens. Having many resource anchors ensures that we will be able to be the best of ourselves in any situation. This is especially important for being able to stay connected to the five key beliefs that we presented in Chapter 4—that our intention is important and worth it, it is possible, that there is an appropriate and effective way to achieve it, that we are capable to do what is needed, that we deserve and are worthy of achieving that intention, and that we have the support and permission from our field of resources.

As a good example of this, in a January 16, 2016, interview, former U.S. President Barak Obama (who was known for being able to keep his cool in some of the most challenging situations) revealed that, for inspiration, he always carried with him some of the keepsakes people had given him since he started running for office. He maintained that they helped him cope on a bad day because they reminded him that "somebody gave me this privilege to work on these issues that are going to affect them." This reconnected him to his vision, mission and passion, giving him the energy and motivation to "get back to work."

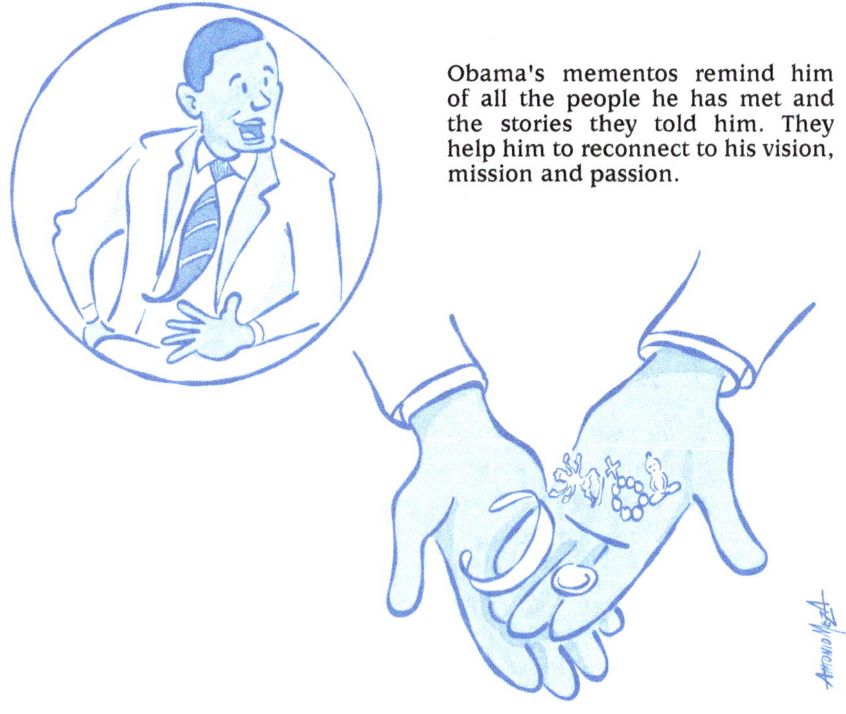

Obama's mementos remind him of all the people he has met and the stories they told him. They help him to reconnect to his vision, mission and passion.

When asked for an example, Obama pulled an intriguing assortment of objects from his right pants pocket including rosary beads from Pope Francis, a tiny Buddha, a metal poker chip he said came from a bald biker with a handlebar mustache he met in Iowa in 2007, a Coptic cross from Ethiopia, and a statuette of God Hanuman. He claimed that when he felt tired or discouraged, reaching into his pocket could help him get over it. While Obama has too many of the mementos to carry all of them around, he remarked "I'll pick out a few things . . . to remind me of all the people I've met along the way and the stories they told me."

Practices for Moving Into Action

Moving into action is the Generative Coaching step that typically most needs to be supported by ongoing practice. **Step 4** is where the Realist takes over from the Dreamer and "the rubber meets the road." Without consistent action, no sustainable change takes place, no matter how inspiring the intention is. In the demonstration with Martha in **Chapter 5**, she talked about the importance of having a daily plan of actions. Making the time to take the actions that move us concretely in the direction of our intentions is frequently a function of time management. Stephen Covey recounts an insightful story of an instructor lecturing on that subject, (***First Things First***, by Stephen Covey, Simon and Schuster, 1994).

At one point the instructor said, "Okay, it's time for a quiz." He reached under the table and pulled out a wide-mouth gallon jar. He set it on the table next to a platter with some fist-sized rocks on it. "How many of those rocks do you think we can get in the jar?", he asked.

After we made our guess, he said, "Okay, let's find out." He set one rock in the jar . . . then another . . . then another. I don't remember how many he got in, but he got the jar full. Then he asked, "Is that jar full?"

Everybody looked at the rocks and said, "Yes".

Then he said, "Ahhh". He reached under the table and pulled out a bucket of gravel. Then he dumped some gravel in and shook the jar and the gravel went in all the little spaces left by the big rocks. Then he grinned and said once more, "Is the jar full?"

By this time, we were on to him. "Probably not," we said.

"Good!" he replied. And he reached under the table and brought out a bucket of sand. He started dumping the sand in and it went in all the little spaces left by the rocks and the gravel. Once more he looked at us and said, "Is the jar full?" "No!" we all roared.

He said, "Good!" and he grabbed a pitcher of water and began to pour it in. He got something like a quart of water in that jar. Then he said, "Well, what's the point?"

Somebody said, "Well, there are gaps, and if you really work at it, you can always fit more into your life."

"No", he said, "that's not the point. The point is this: if you hadn't put these big rocks in first, would you ever have gotten any of them in?"

The "big rocks" in this story represent the key activities in our storyboards that are necessary to achieve our intentions. However, our time is often taken up with the "pebbles" and "sand" of other obligations and habitual actions. If we are truly committed to making the changes necessary to achieve our intentions, we need to have ways to ensure that we fit the necessary actions into our ongoing schedule.

Fitting the "Rocks" into Your Jar

A helpful practice is to start by identifying, "What are the REALLY IMPORTANT "rocks" that you need to be sure are "in your jar" in order to achieve your intention? This is clearly useful to do in conjunction with the *More of/Less of Chart* presented earlier. Moving into action, is always a process of "chunking down" the various aspects of our intention into actionable steps.

To be sure that "the rocks are in the jar first" it is important to be sure time has been allocated for those key activities. One way to help support a new practice is to link it with another activity that is already part of an ongoing routine. Someone might choose the half an hour before dinner because they know they are going to be eating dinner every day at roughly the same time. Robert, for example, goes running every morning. So he will often incorporate new practices into that long-term routine.

As an illustration, we may have a coachee make up a daily chart like the one below and list their existing routine activities (such as breakfast, lunch and dinner). Important new activities (the "rocks") can then be fit in around these reference points, so that they take precedence over the "pebbles" and "sand" of other habits and responsibilities.

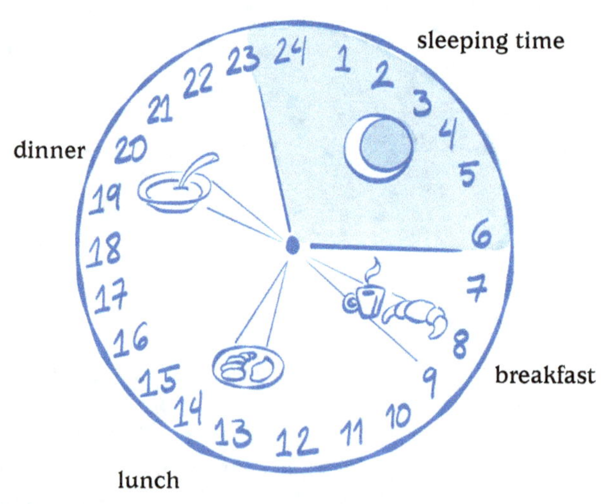

Once a "time allocation" chart like this has been created, the coach and coachee can check whether those actions have indeed been taken. If not, we can look together at what obstacles have gotten in the way.

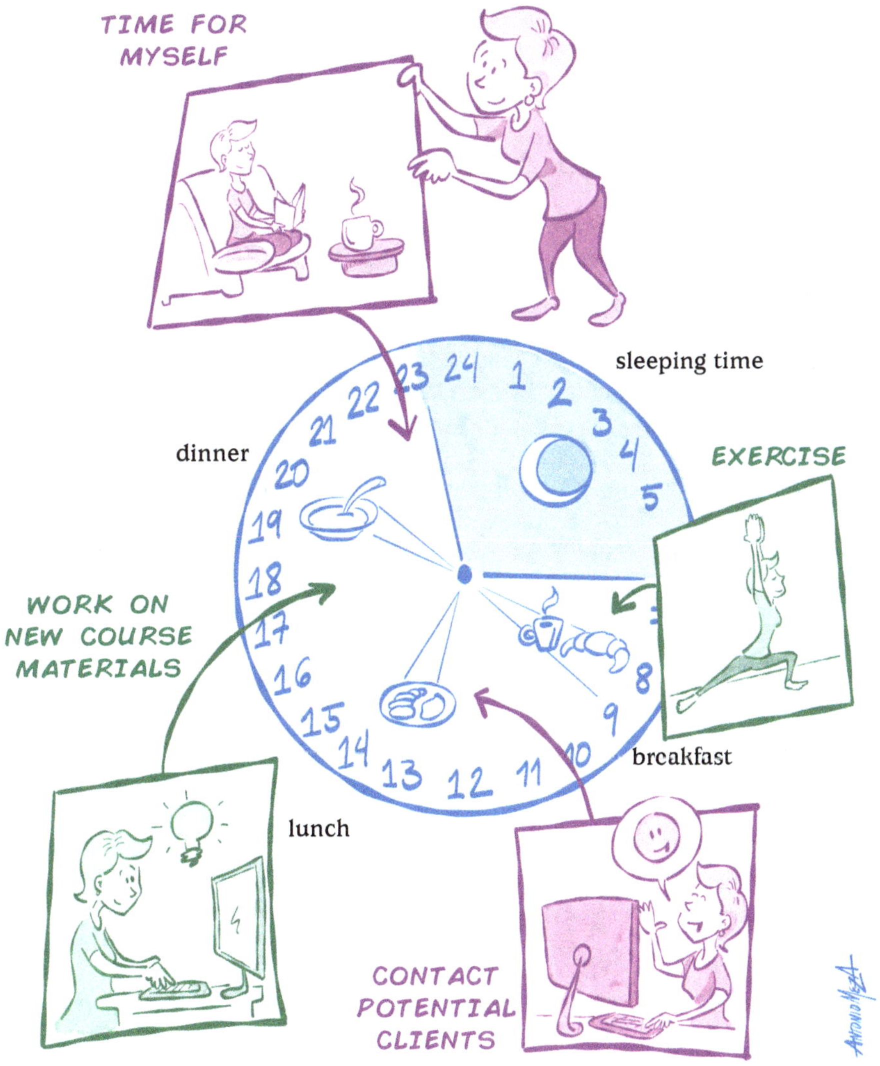

Practices for Transforming Obstacles

Step 5 is another area of the Generative Coaching process that is important to support through practice. Engaging in practices that support the types of inner game and emotional intelligence skills presented in the previous chapter can be particularly crucial. The capacities of self-awareness, self-modeling, self-calibration, self-adjustment and self-anchoring are also useful life skills in addition for being effective to transform obstacles. Practicing the somatic signals to slow down, pause, breathe and center until they become an automatic response to meeting an obstacle can be life-changing (and potentially lifesaving as we saw in the example of the **Miracle on the Hudson**). Of course, the practice of quickly developing a "second skin" can have a significant impact in many situations.

In addition to having a rich assortment of resource anchors, a person's inner game and emotional intelligence can be bolstered by practices that help them to manage their inner level of energy effectively in order to stay within their "inner zone of excellence." As an example, some years ago Robert was facilitating a leadership development project for very high-level managers in a well-known international technology company. This group made up the most profitable division of the organization, worldwide. As they explored the "differences that made a difference" in effective leadership, the man who was in charge of this division made the point that, to him, in addition to providing vision and direction, leadership was essentially the process of bringing proactive energy into his interactions. Regardless of whether it was his team, his organization or a particular meeting, he saw his job as being to bring positive, proactive energy. And of course, to do that, he also needed to deal with the inevitable drops or disturbances of energy that can emerge.

My energy when I start the day

Using my energy through the day

One of the things this leader did as an ongoing practice was that every morning before work, he would bring his attention into his body and feel his inner level of energy. He would subjectively measure this level by holding his hands out in front of himself and feeling the energy between his hands (similar to the process described in the second skin exercise in the previous chapter). Then, he would make the commitment to come home to his family with the same amount of energy at the end of the day. He felt that this commitment was essential to sustain a healthy work-life balance. He had seen too many of his co-workers and employees burn themselves out or damage their family relationships by giving all of their energy to their work and not saving enough for themselves or their families and friends, etc.

To fulfill this commitment required that he be very much in tune with his own level of energy throughout the day. If it dropped, he had ways of increasing it. If it became disturbed, he had strategies for correcting it. If it became blocked he had methods to unblock it or "reset" it.

One of his modalities for dealing with disturbed or negative energy, for instance, was to sing (and he was not a naturally talented "singer"). He related a humorous example of how, when he was going from a particularly difficult meeting to another appointment, he had to warn the taxi driver that he would be singing during the drive because he did not want to begin the next meeting feeling tense and angry.

This top manager's ability to sense, set, and sustain a positive level of body energy clearly required capacities of self-awareness, self-modeling, self-calibration, self-adjustment and self-anchoring. Managing one's energy is a key part of the inner game. We will frequently assign a version of the following prototype for managing energy as a way to help our clients be ready to effectively meet and transform obstacles.

Recharging my energy

Back to my family with a full battery!

Managing Your Energy

1. Tune into your internal level of energy right now. How strong is it? What type of quality does it have? Develop your own way of sensing and measuring your level and quality of energy. Feeling that energy between your hands (like an energy ball) is a common and effective method.

2. Identify several situations where you need to maintain a good level and quality of energy, but sometimes find it difficult or challenging.

3. What are some ways in the past that you have increased, corrected, unblocked or reset your level of energy (i.e., your past energy catalysts)? How could you use them to improve your energy that you feel now and in the challenging situations you have identified?

4. What are some other ways that you can use your body, voice, or other levels of internal success factors (behaviors, thoughts, beliefs, sense of identity, connection to your purpose, etc.) to increase and improve the level and quality of energy you feel now or in the challenging situations you have identified?

My current level of energy

Cosmic Zoom

For clients who are dealing with particularly challenging or toxic situations, in addition to developing and practicing a robust and resilient second skin, we might also suggest that they practice a prototype we call the **Cosmic Zoom**. This process involves taking a progressively farther and bigger perspective, like "zooming" out on camera or a map, until you are viewing something from a very distant perspective. The basic prototype for practice involves the following steps.

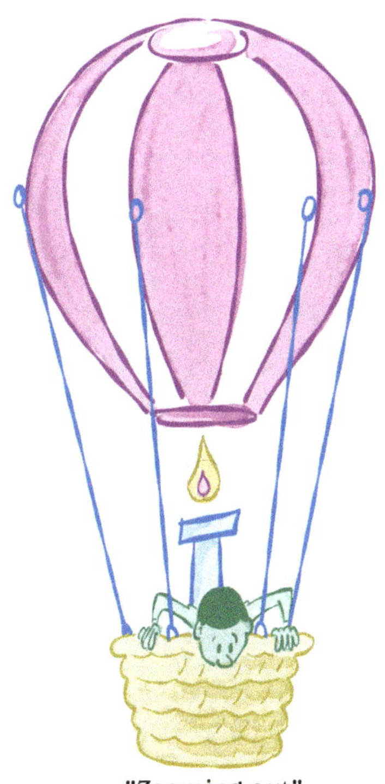

"Zooming out"

1. Re-experience a problem situation involving a challenge, conflict or difficult feeling. Become aware of the thoughts and emotional reactions connected with that situation.

2. Step back from that situation, so that you are observing yourself. Connect into a field of other choices that is "much more" than the problem situation.

3. Now move to a point beyond this bigger perspective and connect into an even larger field of awareness and notice any new understandings or learnings you gain from this point of view.

4. Continue to repeat this process ("zooming out") until you reach a place of deep inner peace and wisdom.

5. Then, re-enter each perspective successively ("zooming back in"), taking with you the awareness and understandings you have gained from broader views. Your experience should be very different when you come back into the original situation. What new choices are available to you?

A challenging situation

Practices for Shifting Your Relationship With Feelings and Thoughts

There are other simple but useful practices that can help to transform obstacles, in the form of either feelings or thoughts, by shifting our relationship with them. One process, inspired by the Sedona Method, involves identifying a difficult feeling that we are struggling with, welcoming it, exploring it, and then practicing letting go of the need to change it by reflecting on the following sequence of questions.

- *Do I want to change the feeling?*

- *Can I let go of wanting to change it?*

- *Is it a want for: Control? Approval? Comfort?*

- *Can I let go of wanting that?*

- *Will I let go of wanting that?*

- *What will allow me to say, "Yes."*

A similar type of practice (inspired by *The Work* of Byron Katie) for working with obstacles in the form of thoughts, involves identifying a thought that is creating some type of CRASH State. This will usually be a limiting belief or thought virus. In conjunction with any other relevant inner game skills, reflect on the following questions.

1. *How do I react, what happens, when I believe that thought?* ("Taste the poison.")

2. *Who am I and how am I in the same situation without that thought?* (Let it go.)

3. *How would I be/think/act if I trusted?* (Replace it.)

Establishing a Practice

As we approach the end of this book, we'd like to have you think about what's going to be your plan of practice. If you have an intention to "become a good generative coach," that means practice. What is it that you want to do and you can do for your own practice, to deepen the changes that you've been learning here to become an effective generative coach?

To create an effective practice for yourself, consider the following steps.

Choosing Your Practice

Think forward three to six months. Reflect upon your current journey and the intention to become a good generative coach.

* *Which step(s) of the Generative Coaching process are most important for you to practice?*

* *What are the practices that you need to put into place in order to achieve them?*

* *What variations of the prototypes presented in this or the previous volumes of **Generative Coaching** would be important for you to do on a regular basis?*

Organizing Your Practice

Put a structure in place to create the discipline necessary to support
the practice:

> * *How often do you need to do it to get the best result?*

> * *What do you need to do or adjust in order to make time for
> this activity?*

> * *How can you connect it to something else that you already do
> regularly?*

> * *Who will help you to stay on track? Who could be your
> "accountability partner"?*

Sustaining Your Practice

Reflect on the structure you have put into place:

> * *How does this practice nurture your being?*

> * *How can you connect it to things that you deeply care
> about?*

> * *In what ways can you fit this activity into your own life
> rhythm?*

> * *Who and what can help you to enhance your enjoyment of
> the activity?*

> * *Who can help you to stay connected to what is deeply import-
> ant to you as you do this activity?*

The Circle

All is a circle within me.

I am ten thousand winters old.

I am as young as a new-born flower.

I am a buffalo in its grave.

I am a tree in bloom.

All is a circle within me.

I have seen the world through an eagle's eyes.

I have seen it through a gopher's hole.

I have seen the world on fire

And the sky without a moon.

All is a circle within me.

I have gone into the world and out again.

I have gone to the edge of the sky.

Now all is at peace within me.

Now all has a place to come home.

From *Spirit Walker*, 1993, by Nancy Wood

Chapter 8

Integrating the Six Steps

As we have done in our previous volumes, we want to conclude with an example of how all six steps flow together. In our Generative Coaching Certification trainings, we end each module with a timed practice session in which we have a five-minute time limit for each of the six steps. This "creative constraint" gives the opportunity to show how the **6 Steps of Generative Coaching** unfold naturally during a session, as there are no prescribed prototypes.

The following is a transcript of such a timed demonstration of the six steps that Robert did virtually during one of our certification trainings. It provides a good illustration of how some of the principles and prototypes we have been exploring in this book might be integrated into an actual coaching session.

Step 1. Open the COACH Field

Nancy: *I'm really happy to be here. Thank you. I feel so lucky.*

Robert: *Great to see you, Nancy. I think it's going to be best for us if we can do this standing.* [Both stand.] *And then maybe doing our COACH State Tai Chi.* [Robert and Nancy make the five gestures of the COACH State together.] *And just a little bit of bouncing to kind of relax and release.* [Robert and Nancy bounce together.] *And Nancy, what else helps you to really come into your COACH State?*

Nancy: *I sometimes imagine myself as a tree and have these roots going deep into the ground, and energy comes through my trunk and then goes up through the branches. And then energy from the space and the sky comes into my leaves and into my trunk. And there, I can sense my center. And I get this grounded contact with it. And then I expand my heart to the world, opening to the world.* [Opens her arm widely.]

Robert: [Mirrors the gesture.] *Wow. I'm curious, as you do that right now, what's the level of your COACH State?*

Nancy: *It's more than nine. It's like nine and a half.* [Smiles broadly.]

Step 2. Set Intention/Goal

Robert: *Okay. Great. I think nine and a half is a good place to set our goal or intention from. So, as you tune into that place at the center of your tree, what is it that you would like to work on creating? What is your intention?*

Nancy: *I want to start with my mission. And I can state that my mission is to awaken the humanity in healthcare.*

Robert: *That's wonderful. Awaken the humanity in healthcare. When you say that, I feel so much resonance with you. Doing things to improve healthcare has been an important part of my mission as well. Is there a particular focus for that that you would like to work on for this coaching session?*

Nancy: *I want to fulfill this mission by doing team coaching in healthcare institutions.*

Robert: *So, "doing team coaching in healthcare institutions." I am impressed that you are able to get five words so quickly.*

Nancy: *Yes, I would like to bring the Generative Coaching approach to teams working in healthcare. I think it could help the healthcare workers as well as their patients.*

Robert: *OK. That seems clear. So, let's find your image for the intention to "do team coaching in healthcare institutions."*

Nancy: *My picture would be this horizontal movement of energy between people, this kind of sharing of energy, where this energy comes through me and through others.*

Robert: *Nice. That is a great image. What is your somatic model?*

Nancy: *It's like it's coming out of me and then goes around to the ground.* [Makes a circular motion with both hands moving out from and then returning to her heart.] *Because I have this feeling that the source of this movement would be me.*

Robert: *Yes. You would need to be the source of the movement, at least at the beginning.* [Mirrors the circular movement.] *How strongly can you feel connected to this intention right now?*

Nancy: *Nine.*

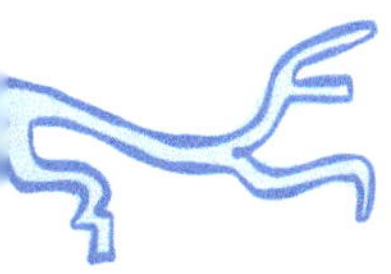

Step 3. Develop a Generative State

Robert: *Awesome. So, Nancy, you have that nine and a half connection to your COACH State and nine to your intention. To develop a generative state, what resources from your field will you need in order to do team coaching in healthcare institutions?*

Nancy: *The first one is a higher power that gives me permission and allows me to do what I do. And the second is the strength of my clan of generations and sister healers standing behind me. And the third is this little butterfly flying around somewhere here* [gestures above her head with her right hand], *which is all about this lightness and playfulness and humor.*

Robert: *So, let's take a moment and welcome all of those resources, this higher power, your clan of ancestors and sisters and the butterfly. Receive their permission, their support, their playfulness. And what would be your gesture for your connection to these resources?*

Nancy: *I'm open to them.* [Opens her arms.] *I accept them.*

Robert: [Mirrors the gesture.] *Wonderful. And let's connect these resources to your intention and to your center.* [Makes a circular motion with both hands moving out from and then returning to his heart.]

Nancy: [Mirrors the gesture.]

Robert: *And, as you do that, check the belief that "this is important, this is worth it."*

Nancy: *Absolutely.*

Robert: *And this is possible.*

Nancy: *Absolutely.*

Robert: *I am capable. With the support of my resources, I can do this.*

Nancy: *Yes.*

Robert: *And I am worthy. It can be my responsibility because I am worthy to take on this mission.*

Nancy: *Yeah, and I have this sensation of "Who, if not me?"*

Step 4. Move into Action

Robert: *Yes. Wonderful. "Who, if not me?" So now, it's time to move into action. Let's start thinking of what some of the steps would be. Let's take a first step toward your desired state on your timeline. [Robert and Nancy take a step forward.]*

Nancy: *As the first step, I need to have a client who has been able to successfully follow this path with me, and I can share their great results with others.*

Robert: *Great. And by when would you want to have achieved that?*

Nancy: *Considering the circumstances, I think that I could start this process in two months. And I have this sensation that the first tangible, measurable results could be seen in four months after starting the process.*

Robert: *Let's take two steps forward on your timeline two months from now and then four months beyond that into those tangible results. [Robert and Nancy take two steps forward.] And how would you know you have achieved those results? See what you would see. Hear what you would hear. Feel what you would feel.*

Nancy: *I can see the leadership team of the hospital and the healthcare institution in this meeting, communicating to each other on a whole new level, brainstorming, and sharing this energy. And they are full of this energy. And they're doing it a totally new different way.*

Robert: *Now, let's take a step back to two months from now when you are starting the process. What is going on there?* [They take a step back.]

Nancy: *I would need to have found my first client. I've been trying for a while but still have not been able to find one. I'm certain I will at some stage, but I haven't found one.*

Robert: *So, let's take a step back to the present. What do you need to do or do more of in order to find that client?* [Robert and Nancy take a step back.]

Nancy: *I think I need to contact my potential clients a lot more.*

Robert: *As you think about this, is there anything that is either getting in your way or anything that is stopping you from contacting potential clients more and finding your first team coaching client?*

Nancy: *First of all, they are really busy. There is always some type of crisis going on. And second, it is about my capability, whether I'm capable enough. Do I have the words to tell them to bring to them this proposal so they would listen?*

Step 5. Transform Obstacles Into Resources

Robert: *So, there's an outer obstacle and an inner obstacle. When you encounter that outer obstacle of their busyness, it triggers some sort of doubt about your ability to communicate your proposal in a way that they would get their attention. So, you are confident in your capability to do the coaching, but not about your ability to propose it to busy healthcare workers. You are concerned that they might not listen.*

Nancy: *Yes. That's right. And somehow that really scares me. As a healthcare professional myself, I know how important it is to be able to work together creatively as a team. I also know how easy it is to be distracted by a crisis and fall back on habits that can have negative consequences for the patient and, ultimately, the team.*

Robert: *So, let's welcome that doubt and that scary feeling. Where you feel it in your body?*

Nancy: *I feel a lot of fear in my belly.*

Robert: *What would be your somatic model for that doubt and fear?*

Nancy: [Folds both arms over her belly.]

Robert: [Mirrors the gesture.] *I am sure that makes sense. There is something there that really needs to be held and heard. Welcome.*

Nancy: *Welcome.*

Robert: *So, now Nancy, I'd like to see if you'd be willing to do a thought experiment with me. We hold those two obstacles there. We welcome both of them. And then step back* [Robert and Nancy take a step back] *and connect deeply to*

that place where you are able to get into your COACH State, which was nine and a half earlier, and those tree roots and opening your heart to the world. [Robert opens his arms widely and Nancy mirrors the gesture.] *And to that intention to bring humanity into healthcare by doing team coaching with healthcare institutions.* [Makes a circular motion with both hands moving out from and then returning to his heart. Nancy makes the same gesture.] *And then let's, especially now, connect to your three resources: this higher power; your clan; and the butterfly.* [Both open their arms.] *Perhaps you even were able to develop a second skin in an earlier practice.*

Nancy: *Yes, I have my second skin.* [Makes sculpting gestures around her body.]

Robert: *Great. So, in this thought experiment, you would hold those obstacles in the field of these bigger resources and your intention to bring humanity into healthcare with that deep knowing of "Who, if not me?"* [Folds both arms over his belly and then opens them widely. Nancy mirrors the two gestures.] *Where are the opportunities here? Becoming very curious to discover what is possible, what comes to you?*

Nancy: [Repeats the two gestures several times and begins to smile.] *What comes to me is that, actually, in a crisis, to be able to communicate creatively as a team is exactly what healthcare institutions need. And it is high time for proposing the things that I want to implement. It's the exact time that they need to implement it. That was about the first obstacle. And for the second, it doesn't look that terrifying anymore. I would just do what I can, and I'll do it several times and do it better and better each and every time.*

Step 6. Practices to Deepen and Sustain the Change

Robert: *I like that mindset. You'll get better and better. And Nancy, in our last couple of minutes, let's explore "What can be your practice?" You have just said that you can "do it better and better each time." You don't have to see it as: "Oh, I tried, and it didn't work." Every proposal is a practice. So, my question to you here would be, because you already are in that process of making calls, "How will you prepare yourself each time before you call?"*

Nancy: *I would connect to my resources and, in the first place, to this higher power. And I want to write as if this higher power is speaking through me and moves my hand and brings this intention through me.*

Robert: *I know that one belief I have is, "If I am truly in the service of this higher power or bigger field, it will guide me. It will not abandon me. It's going to show and speak through me." I love this idea of writing it out. That it is practice.*

Nancy: *I have a friend and she is really good at criticizing, but in a good way. She's a constructive, positive critic. So, I will send her my writings so she would give me some feedback.*

Robert: *So, another resource in your field.*

Nancy: *Yes.*

Robert: *Well, Nancy, I think that sounds like a fantastic plan. And I'm so glad to have you on the same mission with me. And it must be the higher power that chose you for this demonstration. So, I'm feeling like, "Yes!"*

Nancy: *Thank you so much. I'm so happy. I'm so grateful for being here at this demo.*

Robert: *If I was physically with you now, I would high-five you and say, "Yes, you can!"* [Robert and Nancy make high-five gestures toward one another.] *As a last thing Nancy, do you have any feedback for me as a coach for what you found to be effective or useful in helping you?*

Nancy: *Of course, the field that you created, it was magical. It was a pleasure to be there. And interestingly enough, I've been working on this topic all by myself for a long time and, still, during the session, I found new resources in my answers to you during this process. It's magnificent. Obstacles don't have any force or strength when you have this connection to your resource field. And I can feel being able to do that and how that will be my way of doing things in life. Thank you so much. I'm really grateful, and here are my hugs.* [Gives a virtual hug.]

Robert: *Thank you.* [Gives a virtual hug.] *It's been a pleasure to support you in your mission.*

Putting it all together

6. ESTABLISH PRACTICES.

4. MOVE INTO ACTION.

Reflections

In reflecting on this demonstration, we can see that the steps unfolded in a fairly organic fashion. A robust COACH State (nine and a half) leads to a clear intention (easily stated in five words). Connecting this intention to multiple resources (including empowering beliefs) naturally leads to taking concrete actions. This, in turn, brings up potential obstacles. Outer obstacles will bring out any unresolved inner obstacles. That is where the emotional intelligence to hold and honor these inner obstacles and, simultaneously, maintain the three connections of our generative state (**somatic center, intention and field of resources**) supported by the empowering beliefs, creates the possibility of transforming inner obstacles into resources. Effective, high leverage, practices solidify an ecological and integrated movement toward the achievement of the intention. This is one way to characterize the process of Generative Coaching in a nutshell. Of course, there are many variations and adjustments to be made at each step with each unique client.

A key theme in the demonstration was the reference to a "**higher power**." This is a term that can have a multiplicity of meanings. Certainly, a core principle of all generative change is that we are holons that are part of greater holons. The notion of a higher power acknowledges this reality. As Gregory Bateson, one of our mutual mentors, put it:

> *The individual mind is immanent but not only in the body. It is immanent in pathways and messages outside the body; and there is a larger Mind of which the individual mind is only a sub-system. This larger Mind is comparable to God and is perhaps what people mean by 'God,' but it is still immanent in the total interconnected social system and planetary ecology.*

The term "God" is undoubtedly comforting to some and controversial to others. However, we find Bateson's definition of God as a "**larger mind**" that is an emergent property of the holons of our existence is one of the main inspirations for our notion of a bigger "**field of resources**."

Using multiple intelligences to connect to this larger mind or field of resources in a simple and concrete way is one of the most important keys to generative change. Another is to direct that connection toward specific action steps that make a tangible difference in our daily reality. The third is to remain connected to that larger intelligence, ourselves, and our desired state, when we meet the inevitable outer obstacles, and corresponding inner obstacles, that will present themselves as we take action to achieve our desired state.

MY MISSION IS TO AWAKEN THE HUMANITY IN HEALTHCARE.
I'LL DO IT AGAIN AND AGAIN AND BETTER EVERY TIME!
A HIGHER POWER, MY CLAN OF ANCESTORS AND SISTER HEALERS, AND A BUTTERFLY.
DO I HAVE THE RIGHT WORDS?

Conclusion

Thank you for joining us for the third volume of this "journey of creative and sustainable change." We are already working on our fourth and final volume of this series. If you are interested in more in-depth learning about the principles and applications of generative coaching, you may want to consider taking one of our fifteen-day Generative Coaching Certification courses. Certification in Generative Coaching qualifies you for professional membership in the International Association for Generative Change (IAGC) as a "Practitioner of Generative Change in Generative Coaching."

The International Association for Generative Change

We established the International Association for Generative Change in 2013 as a means to build a global community of people who were passionate about exploring, practicing and developing applications of generative change. IAGC is an international association that supports generative change practitioners, training organizations and certification programs throughout the world; providing international standards, a code of ethics and a platform for exchange. The vision at the foundation of IAGC is a world where people around the planet are empowered and awakened to creatively meet the challenges of our time by living the principles of generative change.

The IAGC offers professional membership, associate membership and other resources that promote generative change in personal, professional and organizational contexts. The IAGC website serves as a virtual hub that brings together people from all over the world to meet, exchange, collaborate and develop new applications of generative change work. IAGC also sponsors a yearly international conference that includes master classes, mastermind groups, generative conversations and networking opportunities focused on topics relating to the application of generative change in different areas.

A key goal of the IAGC is to bring principles of generative change to multiple professions. As we pointed out in Chapter 2, there are three main areas of application of generative change work: (1) Generative Coaching, (2) Generative Trance and (3) Generative Change in Business. IAGC was established in order support its members to bring new models and methods to diverse communities and professions. Its ultimate

purpose is to help create a world where coaches, psychotherapists, leaders, teachers, trainers and entrepreneurs facilitate principles and processes of generative change in many contexts: individual change, cultural and cross-cultural change, and systemic change in companies and communities.

To learn more about Generative Coaching Certification programs, the International Association for Generative Change and professional or associate membership go to: http://www.iagc.info

We both also have our separate, yet related, areas of work and development. Steve, for instance, has been developing a body of work called "Creative Mind." Robert has a number of projects that apply Neuro-Linguistic Programming and Success Factor Modeling.

For more information about
Steve's individual activities, go to:
http://www.stephengilligan.com
http://creative-mind.mykajabi.com

For more information about
Robert's individual activities, go to
http://www.robertdilts.com
http://www.diltsstrategygroup.com.

Bibliography

* AP (*Associated Press*). "What Does Obama Carry in His Pocket? Hanuman Statue Among Lucky Charms," Updated: January 16, 2016 4:52 pm IST, https://www.ndtv.com/world-news/what-does-barack-obama-carry-in-his-pocket-find-out-on-youtube-1266454.

* Bateson, G. *Steps to an Ecology of Mind*. New York: Ballantine Books, 1972.

* Bateson, G. *Mind and Nature*. New York: E. P. Dutton, 1979.

* Covey, S. *First Things First*. New York: Simon and Schuster, 1994.

* Dilts, R. and Gilligan, S. *Generative Coaching. Vol. 1. The Journey of Creative and Sustainable Change*. Santa Cruz, CA: International Association for Generative Change, 2021.

* Dilts, R. *From Coach to Awakener*. Santa Cruz, CA: Dilts Strategy Group, 2003.

* Dilts, R. *Success Factor Modeling, Vols. 1-3*. Santa Cruz, CA: Dilts Strategy Group, 2015-2017.

* Dilts, R., Delozier, J., and Bacon Dilts, D. *NLP II: The Next Generation*. Santa Cruz, CA: Dilts Strategy Group, 2010.

* Dilts, R. and McDonald, R. *Tools of the Spirit*. Santa Cruz, CA: Dilts Strategy Group, 1997.

* Dilts, R. *Changing Belief Systems With NLP*. Santa Cruz, CA: Dilts Strategy Group, 1990.

* Dilts, R., Hallbom, T., and Smith, S. *Beliefs: Pathways to Health & Well-Being*. Carmathen, Wales: Crown House Books, 1990, 2012.

* Dilts, R. and DeLozier, J. *Encyclopedia of Systemic Neuro-Linguistic Programming and NLP New Coding*. Santa Cruz, CA: NLP University Press, 2000.

* Dwoskin, H. *The Sedona Method: Your Key to Lasting Happiness, Success, Peace and Emotional Well-Being*. Sedona, AZ: Sedona Press, 2003.

* Gallwey, W. T. *The Inner Game of Tennis: The Classic Guide to the Mental Side of Peak Performance*. New York: Random House, 1974.

* Gallwey, W. T. *The Inner Game of Work: Focus, Learning, Pleasure, and Mobility in the Workplace*. New York: Random House, 2000.

* Gilligan, S. and Dilts, R. *Generative Coaching. Vol. 2. Enriching the Steps of Creative and Sustainable Change.* Santa Cruz: International Association for Generative Change, 2021.

* Gilligan, S. and Dilts, R. *The Hero's Journey: A Voyage of Self-Discovery*. Carmathen, Wales: Crown House Books, 2009.

* Gilligan, S. *Generative Trance: The Experience of Creative Flow.* Carmathen, Wales: Crown House Books, 2012.

* Gilligan, S. *The Courage to Love: Principles and Practices of Self-Relations Psychotherapy*. New York: Norton Professional Books, 1997.

* Gilligan, S. *Therapeutic Trances: The Cooperation Principle in Ericksonian Hypnotherapy*. New York: Brunner/Mazel, Inc.1987.

* Katie, B. with Mitchell, S. *Loving What Is: Four Questions That Can Change Your Life. 2nd ed.* New York: Harmony Books, 2021.

* Koestler, A. *The Act of Creation: A Study of the Conscious and Unconscious in Science and Art*. New York: Macmillan, 1964.

* Moss, R. *The Mandala of Being: Discovering the Power of Awareness*, Novato, CA: New World Library, 2007.

* Sullenberger, C. *Highest Duty: My Search for What Really Matters*. New York: William Morrow. 2009.

* Ware, B. *The Top Five Regrets of the Dying: A Life Transformed by the Dearly Departing*. Carlsbad, CA: Hay House, 2021.

About the Authors

Robert Dilts and Stephen Gilligan

Robert B. Dilts

Robert Dilts has been a developer, author, trainer and consultant in the field of Neuro-Linguistic Programming (NLP)—a model of human behavior, learning and communication—since its creation in 1975 by John Grinder and Richard Bandler. Robert is also co-developer (with his brother John Dilts) of Success Factor Modeling and (with Stephen Gilligan) of the process of Generative Change. A long time student and colleague of both Grinder and Bandler, Robert also studied personally with Milton H. Erickson, M.D., and Gregory Bateson.

In addition to spearheading the applications of NLP to education, creativity, health, and leadership, his personal contributions to the field of NLP include much of the seminal work on the NLP techniques of Strategies and Belief Systems, and the development of what has become known as Systemic NLP. An author of more than thirty books, some of his techniques and models include: Reimprinting, the Disney Imagineering Strategy, Integration of Conflicting Beliefs, Sleight of Mouth Patterns, The Spelling Strategy, The Allergy Technique, Neuro-Logical Levels, The Belief Change Cycle, The SFM Circle of Success and the Six Steps of Generative Coaching (with Stephen Gilligan).

Past corporate clients and sponsors have included Apple Inc., Microsoft, Hewlett-Packard, IBM, Société Générale, Bank of America, The World Bank, Alitalia, Telecom Italia, RAI Italia, Lucasfilms Ltd., Ernst & Young, AT Kearney, Salomon, The American Society for Training and Development, EDHEC Business School and the State Railway of Italy. He has lectured extensively on coaching, leadership, organizational learning and change management, making presentations and keynote addresses for The International Coaching Federation (ICF), HEC Paris, The United Nations, The European Forum for Quality Management, The World Health Organization, The Milton H. Erickson Foundation, Harvard University and the International University of Monaco. In 1997 and 1998, Robert supervised the design of Tools for Living, the behavior management portion of the program used by Weight Watcher's International.

A co-founder of Dilts Strategy Group, Robert is also co-founder of NLP University International, the Institute for Advanced Studies of Health (IASH) and the International Association for Generative Change (IAGC).

Stephen Gilligan, PhD

Stephen Gilligan is a seminal American psychologist who specializes in deep creative change. For over forty years, Dr. Gilligan has practiced therapym abd cointunues to supervise, coach and teach to a worldwide, diverse and multipcultural audience.

As one of the original NLP students at the University of California at Santa Cruz, his mentors were Milton Erickson and' Gregory Bateson. After receiving his doctorate of psychology from Stanford University, Stephen became one of the premier teachers and practitioners of Ericksonian hypnotherapy. This work unfolded into his original approaches of Self-Relations and Generative Self, and then further, in collaboration with Robert Dilts, into Generative Coaching. Different traditions have been updated and integrated into the present Generative Change Work, which includes the applications of Generative Coaching, Generative Psychotherapy, Generative Trance, The Hero's Journey, and Systemic Change work.

His books include Therqpeutic Trances: *The Cooperation Principle in Ericksonian Hypnotherapy; The Courage to Love: Priniciples and Practices of Self-Relations Psychotherapy; The Legacy of Milton H. Erickson: Selected Papers of Stephen Gilligan; Walking in Two Worlds: The Relational Self in Theory, Practice, and Community (with Dvorah Simon); Generative Trance: The Experience of Creative Flow; The Hero's Journey: A Voyage of Self Discovery (with Robert Dilts); and the Generative Coaching series, (co-authored with Robert Dilts).*

Antonio Meza is an architect of vision, supporting entrepreneurs and leaders around the world to communicate complex ideas in a simple and fun way through illustrations, cartoons, animated videos, or through structuring presentations, books, or websites.

A native of Pachuca, Mexico, Antonio holds a degree in Communication Sciences from Fundación Universidad de las Américas Puebla, a masters degree in film studies from Université de Paris 3–Sorbonne Nouvelle, a diploma in Cinema Scriptwriting from the General Society of Writers in Mexico (SOGEM), and a diploma in Documentary Films from France's École Nationale des Métiers de l'Image et du Son (La Fémis). He is also a Master Practitioner and a Trainer of Neuro-Linguistic Programming (NLP), and certified in Generative Coaching and the three levels of the SFM system.

He worked in Mexico as a freelance filmmaker and participated in animated cartoons startups before moving to France where he works as a consultant, coach, and trainer, specializing in storytelling, creative thinking and collective intelligence.

Antonio is also an experienced public speaker and a member of Toastmasters International. In 2015, he was awarded best speaker at the International Speech Contest of District 59, covering South-West Europe, and reached the semifinals at the international level.

He has illustrated sixteen books including the three volumes of the *Success Factor Modeling* series with Robert Dilts, and now the *Generative Coaching* series with Robert Dilts and Stephen Gilligan.

Antonio uses his skills as a cartoonist and trainer to collaborate in seminars, conferences and brainstorming sessions as a graphic facilitator, and to produce animated videos to explain complex information in a clear and fun way.

Antonio lives in Paris with his wife Susanne, his daughter Luz Carmen and his cats *Ronja* and *Atreju*.

For more visit:

www.antoons.net

www.linkedin.com/in/antoniomeza/

Contact Antonio: hola@antoons.net